ISBN 978-1-330-58012-7
PIBN 10016367

1 MONTH OF
FREE
READING

at

www.ForgottenBooks.com

---◇---

By purchasing this book you are eligible for one month membership to ForgottenBooks.com, giving you unlimited access to our entire collection of over 1,000,000 titles via our web site and mobile apps.

To claim your free month visit: www.forgottenbooks.com/free16367

English
Français
Deutsche
Italiano
Español
Português

www.forgottenbooks.com

Mythology Photography **Fiction**
Fishing Christianity **Art** Cooking
Essays Buddhism Freemasonry
Medicine **Biology** Music **Ancient
Egypt** Evolution Carpentry Physics
Dance Geology **Mathematics** Fitness
Shakespeare **Folklore** Yoga Marketing
Confidence Immortality Biographies
Poetry **Psychology** Witchcraft
Electronics Chemistry History **Law**
Accounting **Philosophy** Anthropology
Alchemy Drama Quantum Mechanics
Atheism Sexual Health **Ancient History**
Entrepreneurship Languages Sport
Paleontology Needlework Islam
Metaphysics Investment Archaeology
Parenting Statistics Criminology
Motivational

A RECORD OF FIFTY YEARS WITH ROD AND LINE IN THE VALLEYS OF THE EDEN AND EAMONT; TO WHICH ARE ADDED SOME PRACTICAL NOTES ON FLIES AND TACKLE

BY

WILLIAM NELSON, O.B.E., M.A.

WITH AN INTRODUCTION
SIR ARTHUR ROBINSON, K.C.B., C.B.E.

LONDON
H. F. & G. WITHERBY
326 HIGH HOLBORN, W.C.
1922

INTRODUCTION

IN days not far distant the exile from Westmorland was accustomed to hear expressions of sympathy because he had left behind him the beauties of the Lake Country. It now becomes more generally known that he has a claim to sympathy on other grounds. There is a part of Westmorland outside the Lake District which has an abiding charm and interest of its own. The following chapters deal with that part of Westmorland—the Upper Eden Valley—mainly, but by no means only, from the point of view of the fisherman.

I can claim no inner knowledge of that perplexing art, and must leave it to the expert to appraise the value of the maxims and suggestions contained in the book. From long and intimate knowledge of the writer I shall be surprised if, dealing with a subject of which he has life-long experience, he is not practical in matters of detail and stimulative and suggestive in matters of principle.

The maxim that the fisherman works rather by

touch than sight is weighty. Attractive is the analogy drawn between the touch of the fisherman and the touch of the golfer—the writer can claim to be an expert in both these fields of sport.

These chapters, however, will be seen to make a wider appeal to those who, like myself, have so far forsaken our birthright as to be no more fishermen, but who have long known and loved the Upper Eden Valley. They are indeed instinct with the essential spirit of the Valley. There will be found in that district features so varied as to attract in one way or another all sorts of conditions of men. The fisherman, for whom primarily this book is written, will find the best of sport there, and, with these chapters imprinted on his mind, may hope to succeed even in the vexing days of August. The student of nature will find full scope for his study, whether in the valley itself or in following the becks up to their source in the highest part of the Pennines, or in traversing the quiet spaces above and behind the western summits of these mountains. The lover of history can have no better place for the indulgence of his passion than a country nearly every mile of which has some association with the Border Wars or the stirring times of the Tudors or the Great Civil War. The student of human character will still find in the Valley reliance native to the soil.

Accordingly, I commend these chapters alike as a guide to fishing and as pointing the way to a country which can only be the better loved the better it is known.

A. R.

FOREWORD

THIS book owes its existence to the kindly reception accorded to odd papers on fishing and kindred subjects read to various literary and angling societies.

The first chapter in the book attempts to reproduce the circumstances and atmosphere in which I lived up to the age of twenty-one..

Certain potentially valuable impulses in country-bred lads are touched upon. They are no different in nature, of course, from town lads, but their opportunities in regard both to work and pleasure present a striking contrast. They constantly see their elders doing different kinds of both outdoor and indoor work, and, as soon as ever they are big enough, take a helpful part in it themselves. Nature has endowed them with a faculty for imitation. Their leanings to particular forms of work and pleasure vary considerably. One lad desires above all else to be a good mower with a scythe, another, because he loves horses, to be a ploughman, on the æsthetic side another wants to play the violin, and a fourth in his spare time to be a fisherman. Whatever such natural impulse is, it is all for good, if opportunity for satisfying

9

expression is available. " Bob " comes in here with his technical skill in fishing, and provides for a small group of lads the necessary training which leads to systematic endeavour. His teaching all tends to inculcate the great principles of self-reliance and personal application, from which individual achievement and full satisfaction must spring. He tones down many of the thoughtless destructive impulses of his young disciples, suggesting to them at one time that it is nothing but murder to take small and immature fish, and at another that it is cruel to wantonly rob birds' nests. At the same time he wisely puts something in the place of these undesirable impulses. He is himself passionately devoted to the open air and natural history and constantly brings to the notice of his little band of followers all kinds of interesting things, connected not only with the river but with the fields and woods. However inadequately all this is worked out there can be no doubt that boys coming under such an influence will not only be likely to grow up with a delightful spare time hobby at their finger-ends, but with hearts full of response to all nature's interesting ways and moods.

It is not intended that " Bob " should be understood as a particular individual. He is simply a type that used to be fairly common in the dales—a lover of boys, in skill and character a kind of person to be looked up to, imitated and followed.

In the Westmorland, Cumberland, and North Yorkshire dales fifty years ago it was a common practice for both men and boys in the long winter nights to congregate together round particular kitchen fires. The popular places were those where something interesting was always sure to be afoot, distinct in a way from such usual village haunts as the cobbler's and blacksmith's shops.

I am greatly indebted to Mr R. B. Marston for the loan of a print of Archdeacon Paley, which appeared in the *Fishing Gazette* of April 17th, 1920. Interesting items of this kind are a constant joy to readers of the *Gazette*. This portrait and its history, as written up by Mr Marston, appealed to me as local lore, and so accounts for its inclusion. There are several reasons for reproducing Romney's portrait of Westmorland's most distinguished angler here. The famous Archdeacon was Vicar of Appleby where " Bob's " apprentices began, and some of them continued and hope to end, but not too soon, their fishing. Romney was also a local celebrity.

Paley became Archdeacon of Carlisle in 1782, and sat to George Romney for the portrait here reproduced, in 1789. Mr Marston says there are many references, contemporary and otherwise, to Romney's fine three-quarter length portrait of the writer of the " Evidences of Christianity " as a fisherman. It was engraved as a mezzotint by John Jones, and published in 1792.

Portraits of famous anglers are by no means rare, but, owing to what is universally understood as the retiring character and modesty of the fraternity, few of them had Paley's courage to be painted with the emblem of their hobby in their hands.

There must have been something particularly characteristic of the rugged unconventional north about Paley. It is recorded that he elected to be painted with a fishing rod in his hands. To him the rod was more important than the clothes.

The following interesting passage occurs on pp. 212-13 of the Memoirs of Romney, written by his son, the Rev. John Romney: "When the doctor first came to sit he was accompanied by Dr Law, the Bishop of Clonfert, and, being a man that disregarded externals, his dress was not the most suitable for a picture; he was, therefore, prevailed with to put on the Bishop's hat, and, I believe, his coat also."

I am indebted to Mr Whitehead of Appleby for the photographs facing pages 73, 127, and 141. To Mr Bertram Thomas for those facing pages 121 and 183; also to Mr G. O. Owen for the reproductions from his pictures facing pages 33, 41, 77, 93, and 155.

W. N.

CONTENTS

SUPPLEMENTARY NOTES

WILLIAM PALEY, M.A., ARCHDEACON OF CARLISLE (1743-1805).

LIST OF ILLUSTRATIONS

MAP

15

FISHING IN EDEN

CHAPTER I

BOYHOOD WITH THE ROD

THE counties of Cumberland and Westmorland through which the River Eden flows are not readily realised and understood by the casual visitor. You can seldom travel from point to point as the crow flies. Places are far apart and cannot often be reached without going a long way round. Down the deep centre of the valley you can travel easily by roads that follow mainly the bed of the river. Hamlets on either side nestle in deep hollows right up to the foot of the Pennine Chain of Fells on the east, and to the Lake Mountains on the west. The people of the two counties in the north and east know little of those in the south and west. For many centuries all needs in the way of communication and transport were met by the packhorse tracks across the hills and through remote valleys. Streams were crossed at the shallow waths, and in the more difficult places by narrow hump-backed bridges.

Not much more than fifty years ago, coal was brought in panniers on the backs of fell ponies into the Eden Valley.

Going back fifty years to a time when as lads at school we were playing at soldiers in imitation of the Franco-Prussian War, the people in those counties, and particularly in the Eden Valley, were much more cut off from the world than they are nowadays. The ordinary farmer folk, who constituted the mass of the thin population, seldom went far from home. They knew little or nothing of the great world outside the ring of mountains that enclosed them. Some of the older yeoman still wore knee-breeches and buckled shoes. There were lots of people who had never been in a railway train, and some who had not even seen one. The old post houses of the coaching days still lingered. Daily papers were almost unknown.

It was in this remote part of England that I first threw a fly, and it is almost impossible to set a particular period to that start. Perhaps, however, it had its beginnings as soon as I got into male attire. At that time and in that place we went about in frocks much longer than children of the towns. We could not always get the itinerant tailor to come when we were ready for him. His visit was considered quite an event in family life, for, of course, he was the chief local gossip and carrier of news.

When he arrived there was always a roll of cloth ready for him which had been woven at the little local mill from wool grown on the farm. He used to settle down cross-legged on the large kitchen table and fit us all out. His work took him up to the solitary farms and into the little market towns. He was, therefore, more or less of a travelled man with superior knowledge, and apt on that account to look down on some of his less cosmopolitan countrymen.

A tale he once told at their expense illustrates pretty well the outlook of all those who were not fortunate enough, from an educational point of view, to be itinerant tailors.

Two local men who had never been much away from their own farmsteads had to make a far journey into the neighbouring valley of Ravenstone-dale, and coming suddenly over a hill into sight of Sunbiggin Tarn one of them shouted to the other, " Matt, there's t' sea." " T' sea, man," said Matt, knowing more of geography, " t' sea's twice as big as that."

Occasionally at that time a clever lad gravitated through the ancient Grammar School to the University, and came back, as all Westmorland lads do, knowing something of foreign parts, but still unable to convince old Matt that the sea was more than twice as big as Sunbiggin Tarn.

Whether, however, we finally went up to the University or not we all made our first educational start at the village school, and I remember that few of us cared for the ordinary subjects of elementary education. But the schoolmaster was in advance of his time, and many of the practical things he then taught us are at the present time being advocated as something quite new. The red letter days of real interest were when the top class was taken out to measure fields, stone heaps, haystacks, and occasionally, for the local plasterer, the walls of cottages and farmhouses. Country lads in Westmorland always started to do practical things as soon as they could walk. Practice, in consequence, made a stronger appeal than theory.

Our lives were brimful of interest, and what we lacked in school education was made up for us to a great extent by a practical and useful knowledge, gained outside, of Nature's ways and doings. As farm lads, we were never allowed to be idle if we kept anywhere about the homestead. Every season that came round had its particular form of useful work to be done, and there were always plenty of jobs that lads could do after the age of nine or ten years had been reached. The natural tendency of the young is usually to imitate their elders, and it often proved to be our undoing in regard to freedom. It was always an early ambition amongst us to be able to milk cows; to chop with an axe, and to perch on the top of carts loading either hay or corn; to hoe turnips, and to mow with a scythe. So it generally turned out that we learned to do useful things without suspecting that they would be used against us when we wanted to get away on adventures of our own. But in spite of it all we found a good deal of time to spend in country-boyish ways.

On Saturdays we generally had something quite exciting on, and if any of us had a particularly big job to do at home before starting we generally succeeded in getting some outside help to expedite it. Two of my particular chums, sons of the Parish Clerk, sometimes had a grave to dig before they could get off, and I used to help them. If we did not come on to rock—soft, red sandstone—the day was soon ours. Two of the others were sons of the Miller, and I have frequently been one of a company of at least a dozen lads speeding up the work to be done there. The mill was our wet day playground. The old Miller knew well enough when we wanted to be off, and was sympathetic. He got quite a lot of unpaid work out of us in one way or another, even to the extent of dressing the great granite millstones when they had been jacked out of their beds in winter time. We used also to turn the oats on the mill drying-kiln, with great wooden coal rakes, and it was on this kiln that we occasionally stripped naked and dried our clothes after a fall into the river. We were not much concerned with shrinkage, and our young, growing legs were usually stuck so far through our trousers that an odd inch or two, more or less, shrivelled up on the hot iron floor of the kiln, was not sufficiently noticeable at home to call for parental comment.

Work and play supplemented each other. Too much play might have palled on the mind, although I do not say that we at that time thought so.

There was no Board of Conservators on the Eden then, and one could do pretty much as one liked. In summer time one of our great pleasures was to organise trout-grappling expeditions up the tributary becks of the Eden. We knew every "hold" under sod and stone where good trout lurked, watching through their little doorways for the fish food that came floating down. Stripped to the waist, or with our shirt sleeves rolled up, we jumped from bank to bank and stone to stone,

and tried every " hold." There was not much of
what is known in modern language as " trout-
tickling " in our method of work. If we touched
a fish in its little house we always took good care
to block up the doorway with our hands, and, seiz-
ing it by the gills, soon had it bouncing out far
back on the bank. There was great competition
and racing for the well-known good " holds,"
which were always the abiding places of sizeable
trout. They were like particular runs of the main
river, which the experienced fisherman knows carry
good fish. Take one out to-day and there is
another of pretty much the same size in its place
to-morrow.

There grew up quite unconsciously in our minds
an instinct for good reaches of water, and a dis-
regard for barren stretches, which are common to
both becks and rivers everywhere.

In this way we formed, early in youth, an intuitive
sense of where to fish. We knew also when the
trout were running up the becks in autumn, and
when they were coming down in spring. Some
deep pools in the becks, which could not be
grappled, and carried good fish, we used to spend
laborious hours in diverting into other channels, so
as to dry up the pools and gather up the trout.
There were always signs at certain bends of the

becks of this nefarious system having been practised
before, and I have no doubt our grandfathers and
great-grandfathers could have told tales about
them.

Occasionally we made long expeditions by following up the becks to their sources in the high fells.
We were easily turned aside by any odd adventure
that turned up on the way, such as a rabbit running
under stones, where we knew that by perseverance
and good scouting we could finally get him.
Ravens' and Hawks' nests used to be discovered in
the high crags round High Cup Ghyll, and many a
dangerous climb was taken to get at them.   No harm
ever befell any of us, in spite of the precarious hold
of the limestone on the Pennines.   Lads who had
been let down by a rope to a Jackdaw or other nest
in the cliffs were heroes.   It was in this way that my
friend Richard Kearton, the well-known naturalist,
began his career in the neighbouring Swale Dale.

In winter, when the river and becks were frozen,
we used to enjoy tracking otters and other animals
in the snow.   Foraging by the river, in the woods,
and behind the dyke backs, the tracks of animals
never escaped our notice.   When heated boyish
arguments would arise as to the genus of the track-
maker, if these could not be settled on the spot we
always knew to whom to refer them.

There were few boys of my age and time who could not make and set rabbit snares, or night lines. The latter were occasions for privacy. It was of no use setting night lines in the sight of other lads who might get up earlier in the morning and draw them. But in spite of the greatest possible boy-secrecy someone was occasionally beforehand with us.

The kitchen fire circle on winter nights in Westmorland is the place for hearing local stories and traditions. The talk used not to be of Russia and Germany but of wrestling matches, otter and fox hunts, poaching, of storms and floods, and sheep buried in the snow. Ghost stories also found a place there, where the people were naturally superstitious, and many a time, after listening to them entranced, I have gone shivering to bed without even the consolation of candlelight.

There were places on the road which were well known to be the homes of boggles, and when we passed them on dark nights it was generally at full speed, our clogs sometimes striking fire on the hard cobbles accelerating our speed.

But it was not always story-telling that went on by the fireside. We were often kept busy making things, and there was little we could not do with a pocket knife and a few pieces of string. We made kites and bows and arrows, turnip-lanterns with faces like E. T. Reed's prehistoric men, bird and squirrel cages, and all the thousand and one things we never thought for a moment of buying. The great pleasure to us consisted in finding the material required, whether it was a hockey stick out of the wood, or a piece of tin from the Smith's back-yard, and in carving them and shaping them to our purpose by the firelight. Tin made excellent arrowheads!

And so the apprenticeship went on, and the setting of night lines created an ambition to possess a real fishing-rod and net.

My earliest recollection of actually handling a rod was at old Dick Rudd's door porch. This rod appeared to me to be a wonderful weapon, and of great length, for the top reached to his bedroom window when the butt rested on the paving stones below. Old Dick's cottage still stands, and has not altered much, I suspect, but I notice now that the bedroom window is not above nine or ten measured feet from the ground. His net was nearly as long as his rod, and the idea of Dick being the greatest fisherman of that time lingers in my mind still. He did not appear to do anything else but fish, and there was always an attraction and mystery about him to me as a lad. My eyes used to follow him wistfully as I saw him going off through the woods, and past the weird places for boggles just as night **was** setting in.

This time was the "looking forward" period of boyhood which R. L. Stevenson and W. B. Rands have expressed so well:

"For we are very lucky, with a lamp before the door,
  And Leerie stops to light it as he lights so many more,
  And O, before you hurry up with ladder and with light,
  O Leerie, see a little child and nod to him to-night."
                                        R. L. STEVENSON.

and again:

"I wish I lived in a caravan,
  With a horse to drive like a pedlar man,
  Where he comes from nobody knows,
  Or where he goes to, but on he goes."
                                        W. B. RANDS.

It is all there—The young observer; the realm of fancy, of romance, of great desire. The touch of Dick's rod marked the time for me when bows, arrows, and catapults had to be given up for real things.

I do not remember whether rods were to be bought for money at that time at old Wilson's, the iron-monger's, but I knew that if I could manage to save up enough money for the things that I could not possibly make, that would be enough. So I set about getting to know how such a wonderful thing as a fishing-rod was made, and was told to make the

butt of larch and the top of lancewood.   I managed
to get some larch and a piece of old lancewood gig-
shaft at Willie Brunskill's.   We had a bench and
some tools on the hay-loft, and I spent all my time,
for several weeks, sawing out, and planing to a
taper, my first fishing-rod.

I then took the two parts, of which I was vastly
proud, down to Willie's to splice.   This particular
part of the great undertaking unnerved me.   He
teased me about the top being heavier than the butt,
but finally made the splice for me.   The next thing
required was a long wax-end, and this I got from the
shoe-maker, and was so far set up.   The rings and
the holders were bought at the ironmonger's, and
after another look at old Dick's rod for the spacing,
tied on.

Alas, this was not the end of my preparation to be
a real fisherman.   It was necessary to go off again
foraging for material, and at a neighbouring farm
where there were, and are still, white horses, I
managed to get sufficient hair to set about spinning
a line.   If Hardy's existed at that time, I had not
heard of it, or that such simple things as lines could
be bought for money, even had I possessed it.

Finally, however, the line was made and I
obtained a reel and some hooks by dint of much
saving of pocket money.

I also got leave to fish in Lord Hothfield's water in a rather curious way. The Steward at the Castle was an old gentleman called the Admiral. He used to ride about on a chestnut pony, and often came to visit the dear old Vicar, whose gates were next to my father's and difficult to open. Whenever I saw him coming I used to run and open the gate for him, that he need not get off his horse before reaching the Vicarage door.

One day he stopped and spoke nicely to me, so giving an opportunity of shyly asking leave to fish. The ticket came in a few days, and was the greatest prize I ever received, more than that it continued to come annually for a long time. For the first few years, in the spring, I remember I used to become anxious about this ticket, and would watch for the postman, wondering whether by any chance my name had been missed.

It is sometimes said that people do not value the things they get for nothing, but I know well enough that I set a bigger price on that given piece of cardboard than I do on what I pay for nowadays, and the Castle folk have my fullest gratitude. Licences for using a rod had not then come into vogue.

My first fishing was done in a spate with a worm for bait, and the first bite I had I struck so hard that I snapped the larch butt just below the splice. Old

Willie, who was fishing near me, said, "If thoo strikes like that t' gig shaft itsel' won't be strang enough for tha." I have never broken a rod since, and I am now inclined to think that my first big hook must have caught a root owing to the savage jerk I gave it.

There is evidently something in heredity, for the first time I took my youngest boy out to fish I tackled him up, put him into a deep hole, and sat down behind him to put on a minnow myself. Just as I was in the act of tying I was astonished to get a hard knock on the top of the head, and found it to be a half-pound trout he had thrown over his own, without any thought of waiting for a net. He was as proud as Lucifer, and, in spite of all I said, would set off home, a distance of a mile and a half, to show the monster to his sister. He did not snap his rod, but he forgot to take it home with him. All that mattered was the fish. But I was quite satisfied that the family continuity in angling was established.

CHAPTER II

WHAT was it that made me take so keenly to angling? I imagine it was the result of all these early boyish experiences which fostered self-reliance. One might easily have been discouraged in a remote district where things could not be had in shops, if one had not been brought up to do all sorts of things for oneself, with the corollary that the necessary rod was forthcoming, and the real start made.

In a village community there are no strangers. People all know one another. They are thrown together, however, in certain groups. It was in the church choir that I was brought into association, at a somewhat later date, with a better fisherman than Old Dick. My real apprenticeship to angling, as was the case with several others, began when I got to know " Bob." My voice had just begun to break, which meant that I had been turned out of the choir, and set to blow the organ. " Bob " was, in consequence, anxious that some of us should learn to sing bass and so not be lost to the choir.

We therefore went to him to run over the scales, and his kitchen proved to be the most attractive place I had ever been in.   There were cases of stuffed birds and animals on the walls : a shot gun hung to the big ceiling-beam, and by the side of the mantelpiece an old yeomanry sword.

" Bob " had a way with him entirely attractive to lads, and was full of dry country humour.   His face was typically north country, clean-shaven, with blue eyes and high cheek-bones.   When he was intent on his work his face was full of repose, like the surface of a still lake.   Every now and then it used to break out into ripples, as if stirred by some light breeze. There was never any appearance of storm on that fine face.   " Bob " lived through his days at peace with all men.   All passers-by looked his way, and the cheery, musical, far-carrying voice would ring out a Christian name and pass the time of day—as is the custom amongst people who know one another well. With a few lads around him his cup of happiness seemed to be full.   He was to us the " kindliest creature and tenderest teacher " in all Edendale.

It was our custom to gather round his kitchen fire on winter evenings, when the wild helm blew across the snow-clad Pennines, and watch him tie his flies, and make up his casts for the coming season.

"BOB" AND HIS APPRENTICES.

spring time of his sport with an infectious kind of boyish enthusiasm; an enthusiasm which appealed to us, and made us ever his willing and devoted disciples.

Behind his chair hung an old oak corner-cupboard, originally intended to be the receptacle of the best china, but long ago commandeered for a more useful purpose. It had actually become the sacred treasure-house of birds' wings, gut, and hooks, and all those interesting things that go to make up an angler's store.

Below the cupboard stood a little round table. Here he would sit sorting out from his wings, necks and breasts of birds, the suitable soft feathers for spider flies, and tying them on to his hooks. There were always several pairs of keen young eyes watching every movement, and the strands of newly damped gut or hair, and waxed threads and hooks, were generally waiting for him in one pair of hands or another. At the same time he kept up a running commentary on all that he was doing, and as a particular fly pleased him he would hold it up, and break out into snatches of joyous song. " Ah mun have a bit o' hare's lug on this, and a twist o' yellow silk on that. Ahve aither lost or used up my corn-crake wing. Some o' ye ell hev to try to git me

another.   Ye can driss yer flees on gut at first, lads,
but efter a bit o' practice ye'll come to like hair
better.   It doesn't brek off et shank, and fray like
gut, and it faws leeter on t' watter.   But mind ye,
ye munnet be ower strang et arm.   Let yer wrist
dea 't."

In this way, and by this man, boyish imagination,
always strong, was laid hold of and fired to a white
heat.   " Bob " never wearied us with explanations.
Explaining would have interrupted the sequence of
this kind of education.   He worked and we watched.
Each stage of his work produced in us expectant
anticipation of the next, and was at first nothing less
than a thrilling mystery.

Sometimes, as the evenings wore on, Tony would
turn up with his fiddle, and " Bob " would then put
the fishing-treasures away into the old cupboard, and
tell one of us to put a fresh log on the fire.

The two of them would then begin to play and
sing.   " Bob " had a fine baritone voice, and Tony
the most powerful bass I ever heard.   When the
latter got fairly launched into one of his favourite
songs, such as " The Storm Fiend," all the brass
candlesticks, and the copper lid of the old warming
pan, would rattle like Tom Birbecks triangles in the
fife and drum band.

The impulse to act a part, which is the very life-breath of play, and which earlier on led to the chopping of firewood and the milking of cows, now carried us a step forward into the realm of serious imitation. We used to practise at home all that we had seen " Bob " do at his little vice on the round table. Gradually we got into the way of selecting the right kind of feathers, and whipping them on to suitable hooks. In process of time some of us acquired a set of somewhat similar tools to " Bob's," and I remember particularly how we treasured and compared and polished our tweezers. Feathers and furs were easier to get than suitable tools, and some of them found their way into " Bob's " cupboard as an offering to the God of Fishing.

" Bob " was a man of many parts, and much in request in the little country town when there was anything afoot like a concert, a Band of Hope meeting, or a volunteer drill. So to our infinite sorrow we could not spend quite all the long winter nights with him. But when at home he was not always making flies. Sometimes we would find him either mending or making a rod, not like old Dick's, but lighter, and with a butt of young ash tree. The tops were, however, invariably of lancewood; though I remember he once finished a rod top off with a planed down piece of an old greenheart ramrod. His butt piece was cunningly scraped away from just above the grip, so that it tapered to the middle splice, not unlike a modern " split-cane."

The taking to bits and oiling of the old-fashioned reels was quite a business, and charmed us as much as the modern boy's Meccano. Each connecting spindle had to be carefully unscrewed, and we were given to hold the several parts, and told to remember exactly where they had to go after the drums and plates and centre spindle had been cleaned and oiled.

At another time the wading stockings would have to be carefully tested and patched. We saw at least two wooden panniers made out of the rounded thin sides of old cheese boxes, and afterwards made somewhat similar ones for ourselves. If a member of the Child Study Society could have seen us at this time he would no doubt have agreed with Bret Harte that, in our case at least, and for the moment, the dominant expression of youth was gravity and not playfulness. The pressure of our practical needs, in an all absorbing sport, tended to develop a full examination of all we saw, and special interest led to a habit of concentration on particular objects.

We were not likely ever to forget our apprenticeship with " Bob," for it was close, prolonged, and was served under the stimulus of a powerful interest. There were a thousand and one casual connections in an apprenticeship to fishing, that the watching of " Bob " helped us to link together. Our questioning was not looked upon by him as a " plague to elders."

There were, of course, many little details and operations so puzzling to us that it was only by dint of a good deal of questioning that we could piece them together at all. " Bob " used to talk of inanimate objects as though they were persons, using the pronouns " he " and " she," as is fairly common in the country. He would say of a rod, " She doesn't spring eneugh int' butt," so endowing it with life, and increasing, if possible, our wonder.

I cannot find words to adequately express and picture our master, but in this simple way, and under his influence, we grew up inspired with the conviction that the Vale of Eden, and the folk at large there, were interesting and all sufficient.

It is said that the real artist in either words or paint is he who knows when to stop. Now far be it from me to pretend to any distinction of this kind, but there is one finishing touch I must give to these winter evening experiences.

When " Bob's " wife happened to be out we were wont to wander round the old north country kitchen, and take down from its hook, and actually handle, the old yeomanry sword. We used also

to peer up at the great glass eyes of the stuffed
owls, and " Bob," quick to notice our particular
interests, like the born teacher he was, would grasp
the situation and tell us wonderful stories of their
night habits and sleepy, blinking days.

These were his ways, and we all knew that there
would never be to us another like him.

When some few of us finally became wanderers
beyond the mountain-ringed hollow called home, and
every now and again felt the strong strings, which
" Bob " had woven, pulling us back again to the
old hoofing ground, we knew how hearty the greet-
ing would be when the familiar old thumb-sneck
of his door was lifted. He was entirely unselfish,
and immediately he saw us the blue eyes, under the
beetling brows, would light up as of old, bringing
a fullness into our throats, and checking, for the
moment, responsive utterance. After the first
good day again on the well-known and beloved
stream, and the telling of it at night in the old
haunt, we always realised that our pleasure was his.

It remains but to be said, of this association of
the young with the comparatively old, that the influence of such men as " Bob "—now that the distant
places of the earth have been made near—reaches
out from the old-world villages of England into
the great throbbing towns, and to the far corners

of the wide world. Such men, although they have written no printed books, are remembered and talked about in places of which they themselves neither imagined nor dreamed. These wanderers, often far away, sit round less homely firesides, and, in the flickering flames, conjure up pictures of " Bobs," and rocky headlands with Scotch firs waving over homeland streams; or they go down paths to other rivers which remind them of the old, worn ones upon which they once followed a blue-eyed man.

CHAPTER III

EARLY CASTING PRACTICE

COMING down the steep, old coach road from the south into the village you see, facing you, on a high, rocky and wooded bank, the fine old Norman castle with its square tower.

The Eden flows at the foot of this declivity. If you look over the wall of the ancient churchyard, where " Bob's " and my forefathers sleep, you can just see it away down below. When you stand at the bed of the river you are in a deep and romantic dell. Looking down stream you see on each side red sandstone cliffs, which, in ages past, before the dammed-up river broke through, must have had more than a nodding acquaintance with each other.

Opposite the castle and across the river, runs a narrow strip of green land still called " the butts." As lads we used to vie with one another in recounting the hearsay romance that was associated with this old-world spot. There it was that we played, waded, bathed, and caught minnows and bullheads.

THE OLD CASTING PRACTICE GROUND, APPLEBY CASTLE.

In times of big floods we armed ourselves with long drag poles and caught at the trees and other heavy wreckage that came floating down. The length of this secluded bit of river, from the mill frames to the rocks below, is perhaps about three hundred yards, and was crossed by a long row of stepping-stones. Below them for about two hundred yards ran a beautiful, clean-bottomed stream, deep and black on the far side under the castle bank, and shallowing on our side to a long flattish gravel bed. The nearness of this reach of water to the village, the flat stance obtained on the fine gravel, the sheltered nature of the far bank, the gradually deepening stream from one's feet outward, and the seclusion of the place, all contributed to make it an ideal place for the casting practice of beginners.

We saw that " Bob " could cast across it, searching out the quiet dark-coloured eddies at the other side, and at the same time keeping his line out of the water sufficiently to prevent immediate drag. His cast would fly out from the end of his line, touch the water like thistledown, and linger momentarily over the very places where feeding fish were wont to lie.

Thus was our young ambition again fired. Evening after evening found two or three of us there. All we dearly wanted to do was to cast like

" Bob." There was no thought in our minds at that time of filling panniers. If we happened to hook a trout now and then, all well and good, but we remembered that " Bob " had said: " When yev larned hoo to throw a flee, lads, ah'll tak ye wi' ma to some real fishin'. Ivverbody larns to throw a line here and ah've nea doot it's allus been t' way fra t' time o' Adam."

Was it on all the nights of one long Mid-Victorian summer that I haunted this spot, trying to imitate our hero, or was it on all the free nights of many summers? Looking back now it seems, at any rate, to have taken up quite a large part of my boyish summer-evening lifetime.

Standing quite recently at the edge of the old stream, it did not appear to have altered in any way. The same quiet eddies beckoned to me across it as of yore. I heard the same boyish laughter of a new generation of embryo fishermen above me, and the " caw caw " of the nesting rooks in the Castle Park.

" Bob " would now and then wander down the mill hill to watch us at our practice, and if the back cast struck a wrong note his sensitive ear always caught it. At such times he would say, " Ye'll nivver keep a tail flee on if ye throw a line like Tom Dinsdale cracks his oald bus whip."

" Bob " always insisted on two or three main
principles in casting : namely, keeping the arm well
in to the side; a taut wrist; an upright swing of the
fore-arm from the elbow joint, and a firm grip of
the rod with the thumb up the handle. "Aim at a
yard abune t' watter and give her time as she settles
doon, and doan't click back at end o' t' cast. It's
kittlest time for catchen just as t' flees drop ower
ther heeds. When yev maide yer cast, stiddy a
moment and then keep yer main line straight and
off t' watter by raisen t' point o' yer rod quietly and
followen t' line doon. Some o' ye haven't larned
hoo to pick ye line off t' watter yit. As yer drawen
back ye owt to feel as if t' watter was pullen at t'
other end summat like a catapult. Efter a pull
like that, t' rod-top springs back and taks t' line wi'
it. Just befoor it gits straight back behint ye and
feels as if it was turnen t' corner, bring yer rod
smoothly, but nut ower sharply, back again, and
keep yer rod nearly straight up at turn o' t' cast.
If yer elbow's weel in to yer side ye cannot git ower
far back wi' t' point o' yer rod. T' langer yer line
and t' mair difficult is't to get it off t' watter reet."

And so the practice went on, with here a little
and there a little quaint hint from " Bob," with many
conferences amongst ourselves, and comparisons of
the casting powers of our home-made rods. Judg-

ing from my first Pennell-rod, they were both too
heavy, and too long, but they served their purpose,
and were real treasures in those far-off days.

I do not now remember any rainy dull days then.
My boyish summers were all made of sunshine.
Needless to say, the far bank under the old Norman
fortress finally capitulated to foemen without
waders.   We had caught something of the rhythm
of " Bob's " " swing," and tail flies were no longer a
danger to bare feet on the gravel-bed playground
behind us.   Strong winds were met with stiffened
wrists and shortened lines, and " Bob " began to
suggest journeys to fresh streams and waters
new.

" Bob " was a great believer in individuality in
casting, and used to say to us, after the old gravel bed
days, and when our real fishing had begun, " Git
to know t' length o' line that suits ye best, but ye
can leave t' lang lines to them as knows nea better."

There is something very similar in the swing of
a golf club to the " throw " of a rod.   But all the
great exponents of both games, although they reach
the same ends, exhibit clearly a variety of styles.
In golf the main secret of the champions' power is
control of the ball in all kinds of wind and weather.
They can pick their lie for the next shot, and constant practice has produced in them an intuitive

sense of distance, also that rarest of all golfing attributes, good timing.

So it is with casting a fly. The general principles have all been enumerated over and over again, but good timing is a question of feeling mentally and physically. A firm grip of the handle of the rod is essential, but it is a finger and thumb grip. The sense of feeling conveyed to the brain by a really good modern rod is a wonderful thing. " Bob " always talked about his rod as of a living thing of feminine gender. " She " required delicate handling and intimate knowledge. It is difficult to set down in so many words this actual sense of intimacy with your favourite rod.

As with the course of true love, the way by which to obtain just what one wants in rods does not always run smoothly. Your " lady " must not only be beautiful to look at, but becomingly dressed. The reel and line must suit her figure in weight and proportion. You can then take pleasure in her when she goes out and comes in, and house her properly. She should be treated as precious beyond all ordinary jewels, and guarded as an irreplaceable possession.

It has been suggested already, without any intended presumption of opinion, that the seat of feeling is in the fingers, and it may now be added that this seat of feeling lies particularly in the ends of the two middle fingers. It is not desired, however, to minimise the importance of those two members of the hand which, by their opposition, are said to distinguish man from the monkey. The firmness of the grip on the handle of the rod depends on the tight, clasping crook of the forefinger in opposition to the steady, continuous pressure of the ball of the thumb.

In spite of the "home-madeness" of "Bob's" rods, they were of no use to him unless they satisfied his delicate sense of touch. He took infinite pains in making them for this very reason, and sometimes had to discard a much worked at butt because, by nature, its timber was too obstinate, or crossgrained, to respond to any amount of coaxing.

His rods were spliced, glued, and wrapped together as they were intended to remain. He did not associate rods, as most of us have to do, with train or motor journeys. His rods were always carried full length in his hand to and from his fishing, and one could not but notice that he was playing with them all the way—nervously switching them every now and then in a reminiscent manner. Patting them on the back as much as to say, " Good old dog, you know what we're after; get ready! "

He would say, " It's worth summat to hev a good

memory in fishin'. Ivvery time ah touch mi rod, it seems to tell me lots o' things ah'd hev forgitten withoot it. There's oald Dick noo. He knows mair aboot this beck and what hes to be dune than anybody hereabouts, but he's verra cloase and won't let on what he knows. Ye owt to watch him sometimes and see hoo quietly he creeps up to t' watter and hoo few fish he misses."

All these sayings of " Bob " came out of him as occasion demanded, and partook in no sense of preaching. Like the sound teacher he was, he always worked with us " from the known to the unknown." There was in his voice and manner a touch of the humorous—a kind of bantering quite foreign to ridicule—in face even of the most stupid blunders. It really pleased us to hear his pleasant raillery, and the dialect he used had in its sound a subtle charm which has grown stronger as the years have rolled by. On every visit to the Eden we still find the old tongue spoken in the smithy and the shoe-maker's shop—a sure and certain link with the past and with " Bob."

CHAPTER IV

AN EARLY SPRING DAY WITH " BOB "

AFTER passing through the village of whitewashed houses we turned down to the river through the farmyard, and into the wood, under whose big trees I used to see old Dick so mysteriously disappear on June nights just as dusk was setting in.

Before reaching our fly water we had a good long mile to walk, but I knew " Bob " would be talking all the way and noticing everything. The opening days of spring set the blood of this middle-aged man a-tingling very much in the same way that it affected all the wild things in wood and water.

I shall never forget that glorious morning—*the* red letter day in a long fishing life. The spring sun was shining through the leafless elms and chestnuts, and striking the clean, scaly, russet trunks of the great Scotch firs. Well Bank Wood was alive with the excited, mating twitter of small birds, and the thrushes were singing in the tree tops. Otherwise all was still, and we might well have thought that we were miles away from a busy working world. We met no one, and most likely would not do so until we got back to the village at night.

This was my first real outing with "Bob," and the outcome of the promise that when the rudiments of casting had been mastered he would take me to fresh water. The winter evening apprentice was now on the way to actual practice and felt serenely happy. I remember trying to keep step with him, so imbued was I with the idea of living up to the great honour he was doing me. The consciousness of a certain timing of the master's stride was present, and I noticed how his right foot always seemed to drop into its proper resting-place, as we crossed the rough ditches, without any interruption to the rhythm of his pace.

Shortly we emerged from the old wood into a large, open, rough pasture, where the peewits flew around us, and the curlews rose with swift flight and plaintive cry from the marshy places.

Wild Boar Fell at the southern end of the valley came into view, and "Bob" remarked that, as the night mist was rising to its top, we should have a fine day. "If ivver yer to be a fisherman worth yer saut ye'll hev to ken summat aboot t' weather." It is of no use trying to give expression to "Bob" apart

D

from the dialect. He is only to be realised in his own words, and what is known in the north country as the lilt of them.

He said in regard to early spring fishing that the weather did not matter so much then as later on. "Ah've often hed a real good day when t' sleet and snow was blawen i' mi faice, and mi fingers were so cauld ah could hardly tee on a fresh flee." He talked about the quietness and often of the absence of visible rise of the fish at this time of the year, and before they had got their full strength. " Sometimes ye'll not see a fish risen all t' day through, but ye may be sure they'll be feeden efter t' sun's up at tail et streams and in t' flats. In wild stormy weather t' flees ther feeden on often come doon to them from t' rough streams hauf drooned and under t' watter. It's nea use fishen in t' strang watter at this time o' year."

He spoke about a strong rise of flies, like Duns or March Browns, sometimes occurring during the afternoon in April, and the trout feeding on them voraciously. " If it's March Broons ah put on a Partridge and Orange, and if it's Duns ah put on a Blue Hawk."

" If ye finnd trout are not feedin' et top, which is likely eneugh at this time o' t' year, let yer flees sink and keep a sharp watch on t' line. It'll straighten befoor ye feel owt, but ye mun allus strike quietly doon t' stream baith et seet and touch."

We were almost at our starting point, and stepping over a wide field runner when we saw a dead heron lying in the rushes. "Bob" remarked in passing, "Nivver on any account stoop down to pick up a langneck that isn't dead. They strike straight at yer eyes, and are good shots."

By this time we had arrived at the first of "Bob's" favourite reaches, a long, quiet, gently flowing, flat shallow at our side, and deepening towards the far, high wooded bank to four or five feet of water. He decided that we should both put on a light Snipe at the tail of the cast, a Blue Hawk on the middle dropper, a Partridge and Orange on the top dropper, and that he would start in where we were and fish to the top of Black Scar Dub, and that I could get in at the first flat above him.

"Ye mun use a short line, fish up and across towards t' far bank, and mind ye keep raisen t' point o' yer rod efter t' flees are on t' watter, but doan't click back as ther fawen. Ye'll freeten t' fish if they see a row o' flees trailen ower their heeds. Yer cast mun come doon wi' t' watter, and when it's gitten a yard or twea below ya and beginnin' to trail throw again."

Have you ever seen a novice standing at the side of the tee to watch a great golfer drive off? Well, it was in like manner that I watched " Bob " wade carefully in, and make a few preliminary casts over the water above him. This was carrying out to the letter what he had often told his apprentices. " Nivver alloo yersels, lads, to splash into t' middle et stream reet off. Ye'll often finnd t' trout feeden et edge just where it's shallow and varra tempten to waide. Ye'll be tekken for a toonsman if ye dea that. Them chaps is nivver content without they're up to t' top of ther waiders."

He flicked out several sharp dexterous casts up by the low, near bushes, gradually, at the same time slightly, lengthening his line, and just when he seemed to have satisfied himself on this point, and without, to me, any apparent strike, a trout was drawn quietly into his net. There was next to no sign of disturbance in the water, and very little movement of the body and arms. With a short step upwards and outwards the rhythmic movement of the forearm went on again; so quietly that, if you had not known he was there, he might easily have been mistaken in his faded suit, and at short distance, for a bleached old tree-stump.

Turning away to my own job it struck me forcibly

how much more there was in fishing than the mere casting of a straight line.

On the reach allotted me I managed to get hold of an odd trout or two here and there on the Snipe, and a few annoying smelts on the gay Partridge and Orange. Natural excitement, and too heavy striking, undoubtedly accounted for the loss of several fish, but I was having my first good time and could have stayed where I was all day.

Shortly " Bob " was passing behind me, well back on the bank, and on the way to his next reach, when he shouted, " It's time ye gave them a rist theer noo. Come oot and strike in abune me." The lesson he wanted to teach me was that too con-tinuous flogging of a small stretch of water does not pay. The trout get alarmed, and particularly is this so in the comparatively small upper waters of the Eden when a novice is at work. Since that time, in the larger, lower Eden, I have often spent a whole day in one big stream without unduly alarming the fish.

When I came out, and was following him, a trifle too near his shallow side perhaps, he was at it again. " Keep weel back, it's raither glishy and they'll aither see ye or yer shadow on t' bank." I have often wished since that day that some of the fishermen one meets on the river nowadays

could have had a few early lessons of the kind
from " Bob."

Making, therefore, a wide detour, I crossed at the
stream below the Scar, and waded in as soon as I
could above the deep pool. I know now how
unselfish " Bob " was not to go straight to that
particularly fine stretch himself. In the days that
were to come it was destined to be one of my
choicest reaches.

The take had considerably improved as the early
spring day reached its warmest hours, and I did
much better here than in the flat below where I
wanted to stay. But there was a sharpish wind
blowing in my face from this side, and probably
partly owing to excitement I was putting too much
brute force into the casting, the tail fly in consequence was every now and then, curling back
towards me.

In passing me again " Bob " stopped for a moment,
noticed this, and said, " Yer forcen yer rod ower
much, be a bit quieter in yer throwin' and keep yer
elbow in." With that he went his way again, and
after a short interval I followed to watch him fish a
length of water rather too deep to wade from our
side.

It was a gently flowing, dark piece, with gaps
between the alder bushes along the stretch of its

with a few quick curls of his line behind his head, as if trying to dry it, and then, stepping lightly forward, he dropped his flies on the water above him, at an angle of not more than thirty degrees to the bank, that they might come down well under it. Each cast either hooked a trout or was quickly repeated from gap to gap.

He fished the length without much waste of time, and at the end remarked, " Ye should nivver pass such spots at this time o' t' year if yer fishen up. They doan't tak much time and often carry good fish."

We had now reached the bend of the river opposite the old barn-like church of the neighbouring village, and sat down together to eat our sandwiches. From this corner we could see both up and down the river. " Bob's " big wooden pannier was half full of nice trout, and I proudly opened mine to show him that I had not altogether failed. He picked out two or three of the smallest and explained in his quiet humorous way that they were " raither smaw " and would have been better left in t' watter to grow a bit. " Ah's nut finden any faut wi' ye noo, but some day ye'll come to leuk on t' as murder to tak t' babbys oot o' t' watter in t' spring. If ye tak t' smaw uns at any time thers not much eatin' on them.　But ah's pleased to see yev takken nea smelts.　Live and let live's a good motto, and wi' mun remember t' salmon fishers."

At our feet was a gently flowing pool fed by a strong rough stream from above.　This stream was skirted on our side by a high grassy bank, between which, and the strong middle stream, ran a quiet dark flat for a length of about eighty yards.　On the opposite bank, in the inner bend of the river, was a long gravel bed, skirting both the pool below and the stream above.

As we sat eating our lunch we noticed odd trout just pricking the surface of this stream-flat.　In a few minutes a big rise of March Browns came on below the bank sheltering the flat, and it was soon alive with rising trout.　I wanted at once to be up and at them, but " Bob's " reply was that there was too much of a rise there for fish to see any odd fly we could drop amongst them.　He said, however, that it would be well for him to cross and try them, but that, first of all, he would substitute a Partridge and Orange for his Light Snipe tail fly.

On taking off the Snipe he put it carefully back in his book, remarking that he did not believe in the lazy fashion of sticking odd flies in his hat.　" It's a way o' spoilen good gut."　He then waded over to the other side, at a place where it would have been too deep for me, and began to fish the flat where the big rise was then taking place. Watching him I was surprised to notice that he only got a couple of trout.

Then, leaving the rough stream, he made his way across the inner angle of the bend to the bottom of the pool below. Keeping well back on the bank I followed down to a place opposite his new start, and expressed surprise at the failure above. " Oh ! ye'll get used to that soort a thing in time. Ah think they'll dea summat here wher t' flees are comen doon under t' watter hauf drooned." There was not a ripple to be seen on this lower pool, but the steady quiet flow of deepish water, with a few little ships of white froth on it, showing a quiet pace in the middle, and a slightly more urgent movement towards the outer, deep bend.

" Bob's " intuition, or experience, or whatever one may like to call it, was not at fault. Wading in no more than knee-deep, and fishing almost directly across water, from the bottom to the top of the pool, he caught fish after fish. When he found they were doing so well he called, " Come and tak my plaice and ah'll watch ye." I felt, however, that there was some mystery I could not fathom attached to his method, and that it would be wise to remain a looker-on and await explanations.

When he at last came out, and I questioned him, he replied, " They were takken t' flee under t' top o' t' watter. Ah hed to let me cast sink a bit. Ah know this plaice of old. It isn't first time ahve come across what heppened just noo. Thers lots o' sek like plaices on t' beck, and ye'll mebbe remimber, fra what yev seen, that there are lots o' feeden fish below strang streams at this time o' year that ye can't see brek t' top o' t' watter."

In the meantime I had changed my own tail fly, and we moved farther up, where " Bob " sat down and lit his pipe and watched me get a few more trout behind the island; remarking at the finish that I ought to be quieter in netting my fish. " Doan't show t' net ower much. Stand quietly and hod it riddy for them under t' watter as ye draw them in. Ye should allus dip yer net heed oot o' seet. The hooks are nobbut smaw things and it's better not to scare yer trout wi' t' net. In t' flat spring watter they see ye mair than in t' streams later on, and they'll generally come alang quietly eneugh if yer nut waiving things aboot."

These and many other dictums were of the kind " Bob " employed in the course of his teaching. They were always practical and to the point, and bit so deep, at that time, into an uncrowded memory that recalling them requires no conscious effort.

We were both nature lovers, and the joy of the river itself was but a practical part of our pleasure —even as the chasing on the links of a little white ball. It gave us an object which led us through sun-warmed fields and dark woods, and on to pleasant headlands, where we could rest and look around at the glorious country we called " home."

On the particular day of which I speak, and as we trudged back, the rooks were gathering together in great flocks on the hilly fields. Some fields were black with them, and they appeared to me like a great army standing at attention for the command of its general. We stood watching them for a minute or two, admiring the glossy black of their feathers, and then, the signal being given, perhaps by some old centenarian rook, they all rose together, breaking with loud cawing the curious waiting silence of the moment before, and making straight for their ancient home in the great Ash Trees of the Castle Park.

CHAPTER V

AFTER my first spring outing with " Bob," I did a good deal of fishing alone. I was able to get away across the fields to the river in the morning, and so spent a good proportion of those early days with it practically to myself. The end of each day, however, found me in the old winter haunt under the raftered ceiling of " Bob's " kitchen, " cracking " over with him, and comparing experiences.

We had now got into the month of May. A gradual and subtle change had been taking place in both water and fish, under almost daily observation. The trout, since that first April day already described, had been growing steadily plumper and stronger, on fuller and better fare. Having now got their legs, as it were, they had been quietly and almost imperceptibly on the move upwards from the flats and tails of the streams to the stronger running water.

All the winter ways of nature, as experienced in a north country hamlet, were changing. The dogs

60

began to bark, and the men to shout and whistle excitedly, soon after five o'clock in the morning. There was an early rattle and clatter of milk-pails in the lower part of the house, and the cows were being turned out, lowing for joy, into the now fresh green fields. When the window blinds were drawn up I could always see that the village wives had been astir before me. Every chimney appeared to be giving out that beautifully coloured smoke of the breakfast fire which burns more wood than coal. Sometimes it was going straight up into a clear sky, showing evanescent blue-grey columns against the background of the trees. At other times it would seem to be lingering about in the branches, as if reluctant to quit the quiet homesteads. When the wind blew from the fells, just catching the tops of the houses in this deep sheltered nook of West-Moor or West-Mere land, one could see the smoke being wafted away over the old church tower, and then caught again and again in the varying currents of valley air to be blown here, there, and everywhere. These were infallible signs that it would not be until one got quite away from the hamlet that one would be able to tell whether it was blowing up the river or down, or whether the night mist, lying low on Wild Boar Fell, was staying there or creeping to its top.

This time of the morning "take" was now earlier, excepting when a heavy dew lay on the grass. The peewits were more excited than ever when one passed through the rough pastures farther away from the farms. Here and there one would come across their downy young, lying tight to the ground at one's feet.

Good fishing could also be continued later in the day. Most of the snow broth from the Pennines had been washed away, and the water was warmer, encouraging a new, reedy growth in the marshy places, and the deep edges of the river. Wild cherry bloom was showing here and there in the woods. Sometimes, as one waded behind the low overhanging alder trees, one could pick up in the net little floating balls of what looked like thistle-down heads, with a dash of vermilion in their centres —water-hen chicks, taking their first quiet sail on the bosom of their mother stream.

All kinds of weather had been experienced in the month of April—sun, rain, and storm, and the fells had been white to their lowest slopes on many morn-ings. There had also been plenty of opportunity to study, on the spot, "Bob's" various precepts and methods, and to bring them into actual practice; precepts which fitted both weather and water, and the growing season's changes in the habits of the fish.

Food, strength, growth, temperature of water, habitat; all had been changing. The trees, the bushes, the long grass and reeds at the edges of, and in, the river, were all daily producing more and more fly-food under the warm and life-giving sunshine; all manner and kind of winged and creeping things, that would shortly fill the earth, and be sent out over the waters, each in its appointed time.

Under the water, too, the great work of creation—of new birth and changing forms—was stirring the myriads of wriggling things beneath the stones. The minnows were returning, from their winter homes, down the field-runners and smaller brooks, to the great, pure waters of the Eden, where they could carry out nature's design and " be fruitful and multiply, and fill the seas."

Experience gained by close association with Nature's ways, and by assiduous practice in the art of fishing, began to tell its tale, and our evening talks developed into an exchange of mutual, daily experiences, all of which lifted me, at the same time, on to a higher plane of association with " Bob."

We discussed together the varying sizes and characters of flies; the difference between fishing with hair and gut, and such threadbare theories as " fine and far off." We also considered the reasons which had, in process of time, led successful fishers on the Eden to pin their faith to a few, and particular kind of, flies. Fishing with what is called the " Dry Fly " we had not heard of then, but there was no doubt in our minds that what is called the " Wet Fly " (although this name was also unknown to us) was quite sufficient for the river and becks we fished.   That branch of science which treats of insects called Entomology was also foreign to us.   In practice, however, we did quite a lot of ." butterfly " catching, and examining, in our own unacademic way.

The flies we actually used were as follows :

Light Woodcock and Yellow . . .	Dressed with a small soft feather from under the wing of a woodcock.
Light Snipe and Yellow .	Dressed with a small soft feather from under the wing of a snipe.
Dark Snipe and Purple .	Dressed with a small feather from the top of the wing of a snipe.
Water-hen and Yellow .	Dressed with a small soft feather from under the wing of a water-hen.
Water-hen and Red .	Ditto.
Light Starling and Yellow	Dressed with a small soft feather from under the wing of a starling.
Corncrake . . .	Dressed with a small feather from the top of the wing of a corncrake.

Blue Hawk .   .   . Dressed with a small feather
from the top of the wing
of a merlin, and body with
mole's fur, ribbed with
yellow silk.

Partridge and Orange   . Dressed with a small soft
feather from the neck and
down the back of a part-
ridge.

All dressed on Allcock's No. 14 Hooks.

Fish generally took a fancy to some of these if
the non-entomological makers were not waving their
arms about on the banks, and so plainly telling
them of the schemes which had been prepared for
their undoing under the old corner cupboard.

I was, of course, always a learner, and to " Bob "
teaching seemed to be as much a delightful and
surprising experience as learning. For to him my
stupidity was a delight almost akin to another kind
of learning, and an experience which never seemed
to pall.

We read no fishing books and had actually never
heard of any at that time. It was, as a matter of
fact, not till ten full years after my novitiate with
" Bob " that a friend lent me Mr Stewart's " Practical
Angler."

From all our talks and discussions the inquiring
theorist, whose ways have since become partially
known to me, could, no doubt, have sorted out

E

certain principles.   For instance, that the flies
should be lightly and neatly dressed with carefully
selected feathers from the necks, wings, tails, and
breasts of all kinds of birds, and that the body
dressing (if required at all) could be obtained from
such beasts as hares, rats, and moles; that feathers
should be soft; that hair should be long, round, and
transparent; that gut should be round and fine; that
hair was generally better than gut for fly fishing;
that three flies on a cast were sufficient, and that,
at times, two, farther apart, were better still; that
the shape and size of flies was most important in
facing the question of imitation of natural insects;
that, having discovered the taking fly on a cast, to
promote it immediately to the tail, where it would
be most effective; that spider flies suit the Eden
best; that all the season through there are more flies
resembling the Light Snipe and Water-hen than
anything else on the waters of the Upper Eden;
that the Light Snipe, Partridge and Orange, and
Water-hen, are the most useful in March and April;
that the Light Starling is useful after the beginning
of May; that the Partridge and Orange is a better
general fly on the Eden than the March Brown,
and serves the same purpose.

Further, that, given good power of casting, with
or without, or against, wind, and suitable flies and

tackle, it was all of no use (bearing in mind " Bob's " high standard of attainment) without a useful knowledge of the ways and habits of trout at particular times in the ever-changing fishing season. Even to cast up and across stream, and to follow the old nostrum of keeping your line in the water, was only " touching good medicine " with the tip of the tongue, and quite ineffective unless the whole draught could be taken.

Like all good experts at this kind of sport " Bob " could tell you, in his own way, the why and wherefore of most things, but he could not do for you what he had done for himself—practise. He could tell you to be observant, and you could see he was all that himself, but you had to exercise the faculty yourself, and make the knowledge it brought your own.

There were other fishermen in and out of the locality who seemingly possessed all " Bob's " mechanical skill, but who fell short of him in attainment. And wherein lay the all important difference between them? Was it the result of taking pains? They all took pains. I myself believe that the essential difference lay in the fact that " Bob " took not only pains but the right kind of pains.

He was no genius, but he had developed his ordinary faculties whilst fishing, far more so than

the others, and that this development, coupled with
experience, probably betrays the secret of his
greater success.   There was also manifest in him a
clear intention in all that he said and did.   He
wasted no time on barren water, or in useless effort,
and there was to be found in him an urgency of
desire which is without doubt the mainspring of
achievement.

Other examples of this great principle are to
be found in Mr E. M. Todd, and the late Mr
Stewart.

One occasionally comes across fishermen who are
surprisingly full of knowledge in regard to fishing.
They have made a careful study of it, have read all
the literature about it, and are equipped for it to
the minutest detail, but nevertheless often fail
utterly in regard to achievement.

Does too great an academic knowledge in such
men cramp them in some insidious way?   Whether
it does or not there is in fishing something to be
said for instinct; for the subconscious mind,
untrammelled by too many theories, instinct jumps
quickly, and often unerringly, to the right conclusion.   Learning by doing and seeing goes a long
way, but not all the way.   Witness the caddies who
have followed daily, from youth upward, great
masters such as Harry Vardon.   They all want to

be like him, but only some few, who have an intense desire and the natural instinct, succeed.

I liked to be with " Bob," not only because he was my beau ideal of a fisherman, but because there was in him something else which touched the springs of my being.   He responded instantly to the calls of an environment which was unspoiled, and as God made it.   " There was never a glittering flash-past of a kingfisher, or swift dive of a water-ouzel, that escaped him, and did not add to the pleasure of the river."   Even on off days with the trout—and they come to all of us—he was quite content, prepared for such happenings, and knew that there was good reason for them.   He seemed to forget himself in his faith and purpose, and in the joy of living on that beautiful river.

It is a pleasure to me to recall and visualise " Bob " in those old haunts we both loved so dearly. Others who may read these pages, and have enjoyed a like companionship, will feel the vibration of responsive chords, for fortunately, in this world of ours, there are more " Bobs " than one.

But returning again to my general theme, it should be explained that in those days there were not many day-time fishers on the Upper Eden. Strangers were few and far between, and the local men who took to fishing had to practise the art after

their day's work was done.   As a general rule they
fished with long lines down stream.   Not many of
them waded.   We fished up and across, and waded,
because it was in this way we found we hooked
more fish.   None of us knew, at that time, that the
question of " up " or " down " was debatable.   We
all went our own way, and had plenty of room.

In fishing the bigger Lower Eden, below the foot
of the Eamont, in later years, I have found that
" up " and " down " can be varied according to
circumstances with advantage.   Where the streams
are large the fish are more spread out, and require
more searching for, but they are less easily disturbed
than in the lesser Upper Eden and becks I fished as
a boy.

Practice certainly always preceded theory with us.
In wondering since how much I missed at that time
through lack of printed angling lore I have
been greatly consoled by a scientific friend, who
says that theory always does follow practice, and
that the experience of the engineering shops
furnishes the material for the text-books.   If I had
said to " Bob," " What is your theory of this, that,
and the other? " he would, with all his practical knowledge, have been quite at a loss for an answer.   The
things he did, and the way he fished, were none of
them based on hearsay.   When he got to the water,

and found a particular fly taking, he always had something on his list that he knew from long experience would serve all the purposes of delusive imitation.

Frequently, during the whole of that first real fishing season, I met him on the water, and found that, with certain variations, all the old April maxims held good. We talked together, between the reaches, of these variations, such as the greater difficulty of keeping the line straight in the strong running water, and the advantages on this count to be found in a still further shortening of the line; the greater strength of the fish, and the ways of striking and handling them, etc. He would say, " Throw " (that is cast) " with yer hand, but feel wi' yer fingers, tighten at once and up wi' t' point o' yer rod. Doan't be freetened o' given them t' butt and git them into yer pannier befoor they can git off."

As the season advanced he was a strong advocate of casting often and fishing fast, but not of hurrying, and would say, " They'll be off and on mair noo." This meant that when they were on the most had to be made of the time. " Ye mun mak good use o' yer time. When they're off, sit ye doon, and git riddy for another start."

At such times he examined his cast carefully, but

he never took off a ragged-looking fly that had been accounting for fish, unless the tying was coming undone. He would also tell me stories at these times, and I remember he was very much amused by a gentleman from London who, he said, once went out fishing with him.

"As sean as they were takken, and he gat yan, he was oot t' watter and fetlen up on t' bank wi' a fresh flee er summat, and by t' time he was back again they'd hed their dinners and didn't want any mair o' his fancy flees."

My pursuit of the trout during the whole of that season was constant, and, in consequence, I began to know the best places; so much so that I was, perhaps, as is natural with youth, paying a too undivided attention to them.

One day "Bob" said in his quiet, smiling way, "Ah see yer beginnen to ken t' smittal (infectious) plaices, but doan't git it into yer heed that t' fish nobbet stick to them. Ye maun git to know where they feed 'sometimes' as well as generally."

The lesson he wanted to teach was, of course, the old one, that in sport, as in other affairs of life, the unexpected and irregular often happens, and the man who can find means to meet them is the man who can usually counter most of the chances of the game.

STEPPING STONES FROM JULIAN BOWER TO TEMPLE SOWERBY.

" Bob " was afraid that some day, finding that the " smittal " cupboard was bare, I should be at a loss to know what to do. He used to talk about the difference a breath of wind made in bringing the flies on to the water at certain places.

The glides at the head of streams, usually of a glassy flatness, were favourite places with him, and particularly so when rippled by a breeze. As he approached them it was plain to see that he was wading even more cautiously than in the rough stream below, and manœuvring, as it were, for the advantage over the sharp sight of the fish in regard to both shadow and substance.

The first yard or two of the quickest glide was cast over with exceeding care—just as if he expected to find there something unusually large. You might have thought that, like the Dry Fly man, he had marked his fish and was casting right over him. Moving upwards, with the shallow side of the water on his left hand, he would first of all carefully test that water, where a basking trout might easily be found, and which, when hooked, would roll over, when one would be surprised that its back had not shown out of the water before, for so thin a liquid covering was there over the gravelly bottom.

Veering gradually round he would continue this

searching of the water, and if each quick cast had been able to leave visible marks on the surface there would have been seen radiating lines from **his** stance to a semicircle above him, which would here gradually, as he advanced, bulge to the right across the whole top of the glide.

Above the middle of the glide he would probably hook a still stronger fish, and, with his rod-point up, let it rush down under steady pressure into the stream below, making use of the rush with a quiet, even strain on the line. In a moment or two the semicircle above would be completed below by the trout, before it quite knew what was happening, and owing largely to its own impetus, finding itself on the dry gravel bed. In the glide above all would still be quite serene.

His attention would now be paid to the deep, farther, right-hand edge of the glide, which he would naturally expect to be held by some sturdy old monopolist. Quietly moving forward, and preparing himself with a few preliminary casts, he would finally drop his flies over this best-feed run. If fortune was with him there would ensue, on the part of a still bigger trout, a rapid rush down the heaviest part of the stream. This time the reel would sing, but not like a bicycle over which control had been lost. The guiding hand and turning body would be there, and, with a little more fluster, perhaps, because the big trout found he was being led to destruction, quiet, shallow water would be reached, and "Bob," reeling up, would use his net, not caring to risk a break by trailing so heavy a fish actually out of the water.

Leaving this deep bank "Bob" would again start working rather higher up the shallow side of the same glide, repeating his former tactics, with perhaps a yard or two more line out, right across to the deep edge again. Here, as if by ordered design, other outposts would be held, as of right, by fresh fish, which had not, so far, been alarmed. Any of these, tempted by "Bob's" spiders, would be given shorter shrift still, and very few of them would be allowed, before being netted, to get as far as the rough stream below.

There were long stretches of flattish but gently moving water under woody banks, where the branches of the newly clad trees hung well over the river. One particular stretch of this kind was always a killing place. The water ran deep by the right-hand bank going up, but shallowed gradually to not more than nine or ten inches deep by the left bank, under the trees, at low water. These trees were wych elms, standing on a highish bank with long spreading branches from the very bottom

of their trunks, and quite different to the Dutch
elm with its bare, lower stem.

In May these branches, with their characteristic,
rough-surfaced leaves and numerous catkins, no
doubt harbour a great deal of fly food, and the
trout in bright weather leave the deep far bank
to roam about under them.   The morning sun
shines through these trees cross-wise, and down
the river, so that beneath them the top of the
water is like a dazzling mosaic of light and deep
brown.

Starting at the lower end we used to fish up with
a short line and sideways cast under the branches,
and towards the bank.   Occasionally an erect
position of the body could be kept, but, more
generally, the stretch had to be fished at a half
stoop.

Before making a cast it was necessary to glance
well around, to see where it could travel free.   Such
casts were always kept low, and flicked forward with
the point of the rod.   When a trout was struck it
was necessary to hold it firmly, and to guide it
outwards without getting the rod jammed, or the
line caught in the branches.

" Bob " was an adept in situations of this kind.
They were generally worth the worry and toil of
stooping, and more especially as sometimes, on still

THE LOWER EAMONT AT UDFORD.
(From a painting by G. O. Owen.)

days of strong sunlight, they were the only places to be fished.

From " Bob " I learned to love this kind of fishing. The glamour of the under-tree water appealed to me so much that I often used to stop for a moment or two and admire the tracery of these speckled, sunlit trees. To lose an odd fly or two in the branches was often an added pleasure, affording an excuse and occasion for a short rest at the water's edge, on some of the great gnarled roots of the trees.

I have always considered such places the very fairyland of fishing. The Eden has many of them, and the lower Eamont still more. Apropos of such places I can well remember my first boyish longing for a pair of waders, and the thought of the entrancing spots on the river that would be all my own when I got them. I knew that I should then be able to stand at the flashing kingfisher's front door and take peeps into the dark day-time lair of otters.

The charm of it all still abides with me, and I always have the feeling, as I slide down the grassy bank, through the screen of branches, that I am, for a time, disappearing from the sight of human eyes. Very different are these places from the beaten track of the open well-fished streams. One seldom finds them occupied, and frequently, as one quietly fishes them on hot summer days, a weary,

and perhaps disappointed, brother angler can be
seen through the trees wending his way home.

After leaving these retreats, in the days of my
companionship with " Bob," we always knew where
to find one another. Sometimes we made the low
hoot of the owl, and got the answering call. It was
then that we would ease our pannier straps, and sit
down together in the shade. On such occasions, in
May, we would lazily examine the edges of the water
and the stony banks, for creeper and stone-flies, and
when at length we saw the nymph crawling out we
knew well that, for a time—the time marked by the
great annual feast on these big mouthfuls—our
day-time fly-fishing was at an end.

CHAPTER VI

CREEPER AND STONE-FLY FISHING

THE stone-fly, as fishermen know it, is included in the Plecoptera Order of naturalists, of which there are about twenty-four species in Britain. It is distinguished from the others under the name of Perla bicaudata.

It is, of course, fished as a bait, and some anglers despise bait-fishing. Therefore, in venturing to write about stone-fly fishing, I have had to remind myself of the great diversity of opinion in the world in regard to what is considered good form in all kinds of sport. Not only in sport, but in many other things, there are to be found strange differences of view. Even Tolstoy could discover no merit in Shakespeare, and George Meredith is said to have disparaged Dickens. Remembering all these things, individual faith stands out as a sheet anchor and a sort of reassuring refuge.

But does the stone-fly itself require any form of special pleading? It will probably be agreed all

round that, apart from sport, it is a quite wonderful
work of Creation. One of the species of the great
tribe of insects which is said to be a dominant race,
and the secret of whose success is due to its peculiar
fitness for the life it leads. The pedigree of the
stone-fly takes us back to the most ancient of days.
Fossil remains of their ancestors have been found
in the rocks of the immensely remote carboniferous
period.

Before the great Pennine chain of hills was
formed, and from which the Eden springs, these
insects were strong, pushful creatures. Gilled themselves, and able to live under water for the greater
part of their lives, they probably provided food for
fishes in even those far-off days, and were, in like
manner, provided for themselves according to
Nature's universal plan. We know that upon the
lesser the larger species prey, and that the old drama
of life goes on everywhere.

These insects have withstood all the tremendous
upheavals and changes that the known world has
since gone through, and they still live their short,
strong lives in spite of many enemies, contriving
without any apparent difficulty, to leave behind them
annually good stocks of eggs for succeeding genera-
tions. Their life-cycle is really an epitome of their
ancestral history, and their distribution is world-

wide. In Britain, however, their home is in the stony rivers of the north of England, and in Scotland and Ireland. They are hardly to be found in the more sluggish rivers of the south.

When full-grown—about the middle of April—the nymph begins to crawl out of the water. After he has reached the bank his skin splits down the back, and the winged adult emerges. Leaving what may be justly described as his " suit of armour " behind him he quickly disappears again under any shelter that is handy, but generally speaking the large stones of the gravel beds are the fly-stage habitat, and it is here the eggs are laid.

During the day-time odd flies can be seen fluttering about in awkward flight. At night many of them fly, but whether they take wing by night or by day they never get far from the river of their birth, and often alight on it, where they are quickly swallowed up.

Many of them, too, in crawling carelessly about by the water's edge, get caught by the stream. They dislike water, and as soon as they touch it make frantic efforts to get back to dry land. If it chances to be flat, still water, they often succeed, with a kind of swift glide, or run. Those that touch streamy water in this way have no chance, and are

F

washed down willy nilly—but seldom farther than the first waiting trout.

The female fly is much larger than the male, and has also a greater length of wing—so long in fact that it is a very big mouthful for fish to take in easily from the surface of streams. It is also generally the female which takes venturesome flights abroad. The male fly is smaller, and has very short wings. Some of the males probably do fly, but with the majority the wings are quite useless. The females from head to tip of wing vary from an inch and a quarter to an inch and a half; the males are not more than half these lengths. When the stones on the gravel beds are turned over to secure these flies, the female is much more clumsy in its efforts to crawl away, and neither sex attempt safety in flight.

The creeper, if required for fishing, has to be sought for under the stones of the river beds. It is difficult to see in running water on account of its protective back-colouring, and, as soon as a stone is turned over, darts quickly away for shelter under another.

At the very beginning of the creeper fishing season the nymphs are difficult to get by hand, as most of them are in mid-stream. As the gradual migration to dry land proceeds they are easier to get in this way, and more numerous in one place. But unless for purposes of observation, I never attempt this slow method of securing them. When a supply is required I wade into a suitable, rough stream, holding my net firmly on the bottom, immediately below my right forward foot, and scratch the heel of my brogue across and above it to dislodge the stones. In this way the creepers are momentarily carried off their otherwise wonderfully safe legs, and washed rather against the meshes of the net than into it. To these meshes they cling desperately, and can easily be picked off and canistered.

I have found there is nothing better than a large chip match-box for holding stone-flies. It can be pushed in and out so easily with the finger, both in loading and unloading. If, however, the fishing day is a wet one a more substantial wooden box, made with a similar push-drawer, is better. If a box of this kind is decided upon it should be long and narrow—say about four inches long, two inches wide, and one inch deep. In either loading or unloading these flies you are apt to let out more than you put in, or more than the single one you want to take out, so quick are they. The stone-flies must be kept scrupulously dry, and the box ventilated with small holes, if of wood; though a match-box seems to give sufficient air without special holes.

On the other hand, the aquatic creeper must be kept moist. The pepper castor-shaped tin box, with a small hinged lid, supplied by the tackle shops, is quite suitable. The lid is generally perforated. It is not necessary to keep the creepers actually in water. Some well-damped moss in the bottom of the tin is all that is required.

Anyone commencing to fish with either creeper or stone-fly will be well advised to be careful of his selection of bait.

If either of them are gathered in deeply-shaded mossy parts of the river, or its banks, they will be generally of a very dark body colour. The bright yellow bellied ones are the best.

Both the best creepers and stone-flies are to be found in sunny, open stretches of the river, and on gravel beds. These are generally of a rich light yellow colour under the body, and far more deadly than the dark coloured ones. Besides selecting the yellowest it is also wise to pick the biggest.

Creeper fishing is usually at its best from the beginning of May, and lasts until the nymph has left the water. If the water is low, and the weather bright at the time, excellent baskets of fish can be taken with this bait. By some anglers it is much preferred to the stone-fly. It is tougher and needs less careful and skilled casting than the fly, and the range of suitable water is greater.

The creeper is fished in the strong streams, and the rougher these streams are the better. The rapid runs under banks, by the sides of gravel beds,

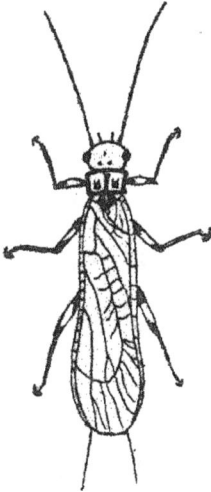

Stone Fly.

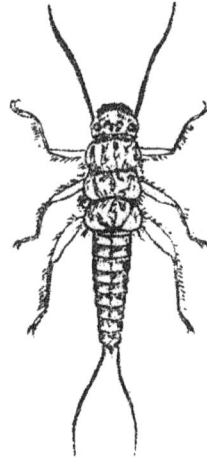

Creeper.

are always very deadly places. If the water happens to be fairly full when the creeper is on its precarious, and often slow, way to dry land, the edges of the river are the places to fish.

This was the case when I fished the Eamont at Whitsuntide last year. After fishing up about a mile and a half I came across two men in the middle of the water, also using creeper. On being asked how they were getting on one of them said, " Very badly," and the other that, " the water **was too** high **for** any sport at all with the creeper." They did not inquire what I had done, but my basket **was** quite heavy. I passed on behind them, throwing straight up with a very short line, and dropping **the** bait not more than a foot from the edge. By **the** time I had reached Brougham I had a full load of beautiful trout!

In creeper fishing the gut-cast need not be more than two yards long, tapered off to 3X fine at the tail. I like, however, to have a short twisted hair tippet between the line and the cast. The creeper tackle, illustrated on another page, **is** made up as described in the text accompanying **the** illustration.

In baiting, the creeper **is** held firmly, back downward, and the lower hook inserted at the **top,** thick end **of** the tail, immediately below the body, and pushed through until the point comes **out** just short of the tip **of** the tail. The **top** hook **is** then put through under the tough skin **of** the thorax, and simply acts as a holder to prevent the bait slipping down the shank **of the** lower hook.

I know several **very** successful creeper fishermen who pin their faith to baiting with the top hook through the tail, so that the head **is** at the bottom. I have tried both ways and found no difference whatever. The fish take them equally well either way, but I find my own method of baiting easier.

It is just possible that with their method and fishing very slowly, the creeper is given a chance of using its legs on the bottom, which it always tries to do; and that Nature's way is then being followed exactly. But fishing quickly, as I do, and in strong water, the creeper seldom has a chance of getting its legs to work, but is rolled over and over in the stream.

In making their way to the bank creepers are now and then caught in the current, and momentarily washed off their feet. It is at such times when the yellow body flashes that the waiting trout seize them most easily. Trout do, however, actually nuzzle among the stones for them, and during the creeper season one may often see where they have been at work.

Stone-fly fishing is altogether different from creeper fishing. It requires much greater nicety of casting, and, in this way, may be likened to dry-fly fishing. Generally speaking the quiet runs below banks, around stones and roots, and in eddies over the main stream, are the places in which sport is to be looked for. Rising fish, however, at the heads and tails of streams should be thrown over. An ordinary ten-feet-six fly rod is probably the most suitable. I have tried longer rods but discarded them. Long rods are too awkward and tiring, and much less accurate than a stiffish, single handed fly rod. A three yards gut-cast tapered to 4X is recommended, but if the wind is very strong and against the fisherman, a shorter cast can be substituted, as the light, big fly is difficult to get out against the wind, and a yard more ordinary line is helpful. In casting there is little danger of flicking off the fly if the swing of the rod is steady and without jerk.

Starting at the lower end of the water to be fished the runs under the banks, and round the big stones, present no particular difficulty if the edges can be waded.

But before proceeding further a very important point in stone-fly fishing should be explained. When I first started this kind of fishing I found that the fish in rising to the large fly, more often than not missed it. Trout seem to gobble the creeper savagely, but suck in the stone-fly. I mentioned this point to " Bob," and, although I never knew him fish this fly, he said at once, " Ye should nip off hauf et wings." This I did with a pair of scissors and the whole business took on quite a different aspect, for, from that day very few fish were missed.

It has been said by a famous angler that trout take stone-fly best when it is half-drowned, and consequently sunk. I like, however, just to see them floating deeply on the top of the water. When the full wings are left on they bob like a cork, and, though risen at, are easily missed. Apart from the above mentioned advantage this method of nipping off half the wings makes casting much easier.

If, as I believe, the trout suck in this fly, time— that is a fraction of a second—must be allowed for the suction to take place before striking. The fish taken are generally big, and need careful but despatchful handling. When the fly is fully " on " —on such rivers as the Eden and its big tributary, the Eamont—you may expect almost every cast to produce sport. The streams do vary, however, and those with fine, sandy bottoms are not very productive. There are two good reasons for this, the first is that very few nymphs have been bred there, and the second that the trout seek good feeding places when this great feast is in progress.

I have often heard it stated locally that lake trout leave Ullswater and take a trip down the Eamont for this particular carnival.

There are edges of deeply running, black looking water which cannot be waded, but which should be fished. Walking on the bank, and keeping the body well down, the fly should be allowed to drop within a few inches of the very edge in such places. Good fish are often waiting there for them, and when struck are quite easy to handle, generally rushing off down, and towards, the middle.

There are also long stretches of water where the river cannot be crossed on account of its deep edges, with running water in the middle, and about three or four feet of oily-looking flat between it and the bank. These are the very places where great sport may be expected, and they are also a fine test in the management of your line.

The feat to be accomplished, if the most is to be made of such places, is to wade up the middle and drop the fly on to the flat, quiet flow near the edge, and without letting the line itself touch the intervening stream. The rod point must, of course, be held well up, and checked, as it were, at the finish.

In stone-fly fishing a tackle similar to that recommended for the creeper is used. (*See illustration and explanatory text.*) This fly is not so tough as the thick-skinned creeper, and therefore needs more care in putting on. If sufficient of the large female are not available put on two of the males, the top one first.

Sometimes it happens that the rivers are very full when the nymph is ready to leave the water. At such times it is immaterial whether you use the creeper or the fly, but nothing but the very edge of the water need be fished. The great gorge on creepers and stone-flies puts the trout off other food, both at the time it is on and for a few days after.

Then it is that night fly and bustard fishing begin on the Eden, and clear water worm in the day-time. But more of these matters anon. We have now come to the end of May, and the trout have reached their best, both in respect of fighting vigour and weight.

CHAPTER VII

NIGHT FLY AND BUSTARD FISHING

Sometimes before, but generally at the end of May, when the day-time fly-fishing begins to go off, night fishing comes on. The time is governed a good deal, on the Eden and Eamont, by the period at which the creeper begins to crawl towards the banks of these rivers.

As soon as this stone-fly nymph is seized with a desire to seek dry land, and cast its suit of armour, the trout are on the watch for it. As it creeps from stone to stone on its perilous path, it occasionally gets washed off its feet, and it is at such times that the trout seize it. The taste of this big, luscious morsel seems to put the trout off ordinary small fly food for the time being, and, on account of the great gorge it provides, even for a few days after it is over.

THE LOWER EAMONT FACING CROSS FELL.

If the spring is warm and fine, without any cold floods, creepers are often to be found in trout by the middle of April. When this is the case the fly fisherman begins to shake his head, and tells you that he knows why he has not been doing so well as he expected.

A cold, wet spring retards the migration of the creepers. The water is too heavy for successful movements landwards, and its temperature probably not high enough to give sufficient strength to the instinctive, annual impulse. But, whether the spring is warm or cold, as soon as the trout get a mouthful of either the nymph or fly they will not pay much further attention to the small, artificial flies that are cast over them.

Then it is that the local anglers, at any rate, start their night fishing. Many of them use the small day-time flies during the whole of the night fishing season, which lasts, at its very best, until the end of June. Commencing at dusk they confine their attention to the flattish water at the tails of streams, and to places where there is a long, deepish stretch approachable by easy wading from one shallowing side.

Every fisherman of this kind has his favourite night haunt, and sometimes two or three of similar taste will fish the same piece of water, perhaps not more than forty or fifty yards apart. I have known night fishers who would walk two or three miles in order to fish a favourite reach.

They all, of course, try to choose water that has been previously productive of good results. This is the particular feature of the special choice, but fishermen vary in daring, and the nervous wader is not likely to choose a reach where the dark night wading is too risky, however good otherwise it may be. It can be taken for granted that they all know the water well, and in this respect hold a considerable advantage over the visitor angler.

On a really good night, when once the fisherman has got into his pool, it is not necessary to move about much to make a good catch. If there is a moon, and he has taken his stand under the shadow of a tree, or a small row of trees, he remains there.

Many night fishermen pin their faith to what is known on the Eden as a bustard (moth). They are generally made from the primary wing feathers of brown and white owls. The bodies of brown bustards are sometimes of a much darker brown than the darkest part of the feathers, and sometimes orange coloured. Occasionally a piece of soft washleather is tied into the body part, to project about three-sixteenths of an inch as a waggly tail.

The white bustards have a white body and black head. These two colours are the general favourites, but an all-red bustard is sometimes used, and this is dressed from the dyed primary feather of a white owl.

The ordinary flies generally used at night are Light Woodcock and Yellow, Light Snipe and Yellow, Water-hen and Red, Light Starling and Yellow, Corncrake, and Water-hen and Yellow.

Whether the fisherman uses flies or bustards he does not, as a usual practice, put on more than one dropper, and sometimes a bustard point is used with an ordinary fly dropper. The night fisherman has three distinct advantages in his favour; the trout take very little notice of him, he can use a short line, and his cast can be of stronger gut.

If the fish are feeding well they are not readily "put down" at night, and when they are hooked the stronger cast allows of despatchful netting, particularly if a larger-hooked bustard is taken. Fishing is often carried on in June till three or four o'clock in the morning, but when the season has advanced into July and August the time of the take does not last much more than, at the most,

a couple of hours, beginning just as dusk is
setting in.

Night fishing does not appeal to everybody, but
some of its devotees take more delight in it than any
other kind of sport with the rod.

This is so with an old friend whose boyhood was
contemporaneous with my own, and who is actually
a first-rate, all-round fisher. His favourite bustard
is a brown owl with a dark brown body and a little
red hackle.

This same angler had an unusual experience one
night when only a lad of eighteen years. He says,
" Boy-like I had four bustards on instead of the
usual two, and was suddenly surprised to find that
they had all been taken. On the tail fly was a pound
chub. This, as usual, made no great fight, and very
soon went swimming quietly about, so that each of
the droppers was taken in turn, and much to my
astonishment I netted the lot."

Night fishing has never appealed to me in spite
of the large baskets of fish that are taken in this
way. I have practised it occasionally all my life,
but I cannot say that it has afforded me anything
like the enjoyment of day-time fishing. Sometimes
when I have been upon the Eden, in June, with
angling friends I have seen very little of them for
a week at a time. They were in bed when I was

out enjoying the river, with all the full, day-time delights of its banks and braes.

One night, when a trifle younger than my friend of the " catch of four," and I had been to " Bob " to get my hair cut, he persuaded me to go out night fishing with him for the first time.

We had to walk a mile and a half to our reach, through the great, old wood, to the starting place of that first day's spring fishing already described. Spring fishing and night fishing have this in common that the trout are to be found in similar water. The great fields on our side were lying flat and still in the subtle shade of evening light, and the woods on the far bank showed dark to the edge of the river, with a quickly paling western light through the tops of the trees. As we walked along I had the feeling that very soon we should be shut in by the night.

Already the screech and hoot of the stirring night owls could be heard, and the distant sound of barking, farmyard dogs. Now and again the clatter of a gate reached the ear, conveying to the mind the finish of the day. Corncrakes, every now and then, gave out their harsh crake at our feet, and, seemingly, but for these early night sounds of the wild we were entirely alone.

We started our fishing about fifty yards apart.

G

Both of us knew every inch of the water, and, whereas I was aware of a certain uncanny feeling of timidity in stepping into the dark water, "Bob" proceeded as if it had been broad daylight and second nature to him.

I could hear the regular clock-like swish of his line, and knew exactly where he was below me, but could not see him. Trout were rising all around me, steadily and quietly.

The water, for a few yards in front of my rod, retained on its surface all through the night a flat glimmer of light. For some time I kept on, and fish took me without any fear, but as the night wore on the weird sounds increased, and impinged on the ear with a new and strange distinctness.

Every now and then a weasel or stoat would take nature's legitimate toll of some poor rabbit, and the still night would be awakened by a shrill scream. The succeeding stillness was even more uncanny than these occasional, murderous sounds.

Finally, as if to complete my uneasiness, there came a great, ominous splash just above me, and, able to bear it no longer, I shouted to "Bob" to ask him if he had heard it. His answer came back immediately, "Ga on wi' thi fishen, it's nobbut a coo wanten a drink." It was reassuring to hear his voice, and feel that he was near by in the darkness, for the cow made even more noise in getting out than in, and ended by lying down on the bank with a deep groan.

As the night wore on and I thought that " Bob " would never stop, I contrasted all this with our mutual day-time pleasure, and knew that our joys could seldom be shared in the night watches.

Finally he came out satisfied, lit his pipe, and we walked home through the long wood. I stumbled and almost fell every now and then, but he, to my infinite wonder, sailed gaily on, never faltering, as though possessed of cat's eyes.

In spite of the great love I had for our hero he never succeeded in making an ardent night fisher of me. The memory of that first experience remains with me still, and although I have frequently gone out since it has never been for more than a couple of hours.

The lower Eamont, where I have often stayed in a delightful old farmhouse close to the stream, has always drawn me at night-time more than the Eden, but what with tangled lines and other discomforts of the dark, it has not been the way with me to look forward with any particular kind of joy to the catches that can be made when the sun has gone down.

So without in any way wishing to disparage night

fishing, it can be truthfully said that " Might is Right with the creatures of Night," whether they be two or four footed, and personally I prefer the morning, when " the network of sun-flecked shadow rings on another note."

CHAPTER VIII

CLEAR WATER WORM FISHING

THE first Jubilee year—1887—was extraordinarily dry. From the end of May, onwards for three months, hardly any rain fell. That was the year of an exceptionally long holiday for me, beginning about the middle of June.

On the evening of the Jubilee day large bonfires were lit on all the old beacon-tops of the Cumbrian Hills and Pennine Fells. The bonfire on the top of Cross Fell, the highest point of the Pennine Chain, set Lord Hothfield's grouse moors ablaze, and an immense area of heather was burnt off. Everything was as dry as tinder, and even the bracken on the fells paled and withered long before its usual time.

The Eden could be crossed in hitherto unwadeable places. In getting into the river and coming out one had to be careful not to step on wasps' nests. We used to rob these with cyanide of potassium, and the rounds of comb taken were often

as big as the copper bowl of Bob's warming pan.
The wasp grubs were used as bait for chub, which
were plentiful in some deep pools of the river, and
could be seen that year sailing about in shoals.
But we soon tired of that kind of kill-time sport.

One evening whilst we were sitting by the river,
after a baking-hot day, watching the swifts at their
shrill play, Bob remarked, " There's nowt for ye
to dea but start that new fangled dodge of ' runnen
worm.' " He had no thought of trying it himself,
had given up all idea of good water that year, and
thought I had better get to work at something before
my next exile to town. It was a habit of his to
sympathise with me in my forced absences from the
river.

Although neither of us knew anything about
" runnen worm " " Bob " at least thought our
knowledge of the river was enough for an attempt.

So we borrowed a friend's copy of " Stewart," and
set about making a long, light, double-handed rod
out of sundry discarded old butts and tops.
Stewart's directions were followed very carefully,
and the well-known three hook tackles were soon
ready.

The dry weather had been too much for the
worms, and all ordinary places such as kitchen
gardens were drawn blank. Finally we found

exactly what we wanted at the bottom of a tip of road-sweepings and decayed leaves. In the course of a few days the worms were scoured bright in soft moss, and were as lively when touched as steel springs.

After all the years that have passed I cannot quite remember the details of that first hot day with upstream worm, but I can certainly remember covering a lot of ground, and finding myself some miles away from home at tea-time. Sufficient trout were caught, however, to warrant further effort, and, in the evening, we made sundry alterations to tackle and bait as suggested by the day's experience.

Both the size of the hooks and the distance between them were lessened. All the bigger worms were discarded, and the bag filled with inch-and-half ones. Missing one day I was up betimes on the next, and on the water soon after eight o'clock.

Upon this occasion things went much better, and I began to realise that " up and across " was better generally than " straight up," also that the trout were quite fond of those bright, lively little worms, if they saw them coming quietly down past their doorways under the streamy banks, and the top-side of large stones.

I also found that, if I faced the sun (and morning fishing up the Eden allows of that) trout were to be found basking in the thin rippling water at the heads and sides of streams, as well as under the banks. The worm was thrown with a shortish line into all the likely places above me, and immediately it stopped, or there was a slight pull, striking began. In this way the nefarious art—if the qualifying word is preferred—was acquired, and several neighbouring frying-pans began to do their duty again, in spite of blazing sun and brown hillsides.

" Bob " was right. The fine weather held up during the whole of that long holiday. Distant thunder was occasionally heard from the fells, and odd showers could be seen travelling along their tops, but they all passed away like mountain mist in a wind, without adding a drop to the parched river feeders below.

Clear water worm fishing undoubtedly depends for its success on a sound working knowledge of the ways of trout in times of low water, and on quick fishing of the suitable reaches. The slow order of fishermen will never fill panniers. Wading upstream and passing smartly from one suitable reach to another requires a good deal of exertion, and one seldom finds a fisherman who is prepared to go the pace required under a broiling sun.

What makes this kind of fishing so deadly, when practised by the fisherman who is acquainted with the low water habits of trout, is that he knows exactly where to find them. They are congregated together in narrowed streams. The river and becks are like an open book to such a man. From the page of contents he can make his sure selection, and skip the unwanted chapters. He ensures success by covering the suitable ground quickly at the time of the take, which is generally between an early breakfast and mid-afternoon.

From that first dry year mentioned I have fished the upstream worm, off and on, with a satisfying measure of success when other methods were out of the question.

My greatest day was probably in 1889. I remember it distinctly as my last summer day on the Eden that year, for on the next I went off to Sweden for a couple of months. It was the day before the assizes, and the proprietor of the leading hotel, to whom I was indebted for many past favours, told me he could get no fish for the sheriff and his retinue.

I set off, therefore, with the strong desire to requite him. The trout were in a taking mood, and all the conditions ideal. The long, two-handed rod had been discarded for a less clumsy and much more enjoyable Hardy " Pennell." I found things waiting for me almost as though the trout had

known the sheriff could not sit down to dinner without fish.

By soon after twelve o'clock the strap was biting
into my shoulder, and I was glad to turn out the
contents of the pannier into a butter bowl at a farm,
to be called for later on. Between three and four
it was getting heavy again, and the great day came
to a glorious end with the capture of a three-and-
a-half pounder—the bonniest fish I have ever
caught, before or since.

On getting home I emptied the take of nineteen
and a half pounds into a favourite old butter basket
of my mother's, and sent them down to my friend
in good time for his evening guests.

Thereby hangs a tale, which I must perforce tell,
even at the risk of being considered tedious. About
a year later the aforesaid proprietor called on my
mother to say that he was putting up for election
as a town councillor, and that he hoped he might
rely on her vote. She replied that he could have it
provided he returned the old butter basket which
had been sent with that catch twelve months before.

Worming I consider justifiable under the conditions named, but it is not in any sense to be confused
with worming in a spate; and beyond a knowledge of
the habits of trout it requires, for its successful
practice, nicety of casting; skill at keeping out of

sight; careful selection of suitable water; judicious wading; and painstaking preparation of the bait.

The gut cast should be three yards long and tapered to 3X. A light line is often advised, but personally I prefer the same line I use for fly—a Hardy Corona. Too fine a line, with a long, gut cast at the end of it, is difficult to manage, as there are seldom more than sixteen to eighteen feet out, including the cast. Moreover, the line should be kept out of the water as much as possible, and, frequently, the top-end of the gut cast itself.

In casting a well-scoured worm there is no necessity whatever to be ladylike. Naturally one is conscious that the worm is there, but otherwise the throw can be made as when fly fishing, by dropping the rod-point a trifle nearer the water, and recovering the floating line by raising it gradually, until the downward flow of the worm has completed its natural course.

Pause a moment after the worm alights, and if, in spite of this, your rod-point jerks back at the finish discard it, and use something stiffer. Once, when fishing with a friend, we saw fish rising in still, deepish water, under trees. As an experiment I cast a worm amongst them, and, when it touched the water, I kept my hand quite still without any attempt being made to raise the rod. This worm

was taken.   The dodge has often accounted **for**
similar odd rising fish in shady places, but never
if the slightest attempt to lift the line was made.
So the point is to avoid drag at all costs.

In regard to the tackle itself I have always found,
excepting in the becks, three hooks the best.   If
they are whipped on to fine 3X gut a lively,
toughened worm, when pricked, frequently curls
itself up into a knot, and has to be removed.   The
tackle is, therefore, better when it **is** dressed **on** a
stiff piece of gut with the top hook eyed.   This
prevents the knotting up of the worm.   (*See
illustration.*)

When a tackle of this kind is worn out and coming
undone, or is lost when fishing, it is an easy matter
to tie on another to the end of the cast, as the gut
is already damped with use in the water.

Another very important point to remember is not
to bait the three hooks in such a way **as** to allow
of the worm showing a series of unnatural-looking
loops.   Stewart's illustration shows this fault.   It
has been found from careful experiment that trout
take a fairly straight worm best.   When a worm **is**
dropped into a glass tank containing trout they take
it when it straightens out.   Put on the worm from
the head downwards, leaving very little " spare "
at both head and tail.

On no account must sinkers be used. Worms without knots in the middle are best. Brandlings and red leaf-mould worms are too soft. The small worms of about one and three quarter inches long, found in gardens and old road sweepings, are quite suitable. When well secured in sphagnum moss they turn to a bright, lightish colour. Some fisher-men keep a heap of garden soil in a shady corner, into which potato peelings are thrown. The worms bred in this way are excellent. Ordinary hedgerow moss is not so good as sphagnum. It is too coarse, and full of sharp bits of grass and sticks.

A good receptacle to scour worms in is a large, corked flower-pot. It should be filled with sphag-num, and the worms, when washed, dropped into it. The moss should be soaked in water and then wrung out, leaving just sufficient moisture in it to keep the receptacle cool. This done, a piece of old canvas can be tied across the top, and the pot placed in a shady corner of the garden. If a good deal of this kind of fishing is contemplated two pots should be kept going. When one has been used up clean it out well, and put in fresh moss. If these instructions are followed worm fishing is not by any means a dirty business.

When setting off for a day's fishing in hot weather two little flannel bags are necessary; one to contain the main worm supply, and the other to carry a few for immediate use. Both should have fresh damp sphagnum in them.

In practising this somewhat special art of fishing start at the bottom of your length, and, without neglecting any of the streams, runs under banks and walls, and bridges, or rippled, thin water at the heads of streams, make haste in orderly fashion. On dullish summer days the trout will be in the neighbourhood of the streams. In hot glaring weather many of them will be found in the thin-water flats at the tops of the streams, and, if it happens to be rippled, and one approaches it properly, there sport will be good.

Narrow, streamy glides past gravel beds, with shady deeps on the far side, are ideal places. But in approaching these on bright days, the thin water within a foot of the edge should provide the first cast. Supposing the thin edge to be on your right,, keep well below it, and cast directly up, only allowing the gut cast, or even part of it, to touch the water. Then follow with a cast to the left into the middle of the run, and another right under the deep, and perhaps, bushy bank. A horizontal, forehand cast is best under such banks, the worm should be placed well in, and the rod-point kept down to clear the branches. This is generally a very deadly cast, and often finds the haunt of an extra large trout or two.

Rivers flowing in a southerly direction are difficult to fish in the sunny summer months. Fishing them down exposes you to the upward glance of the trout, and fishing upstream shows the tell-tale shadows of both moving rod and standing fisherman.

Even the Eamont, which I know so well, is much more difficult to fish than the northerly flowing Eden. It leaves Ullswater flowing almost directly east. Fishing it up from the point at which it enters the Eden the morning sun is mainly at your back, with a gradual veer to your left side. But it is very woody, and runs below deepish banks. Some of its beautiful streams run under archways of tree branches, with the sun only striking the water in dazzling patches. These bowered river groves are delightful places to fish on sunny June and July days. Wading up them you are in a very fairy-land of colour.

Such glades can be fished unseen, but, to the fisherman with the seeing eye, Nature is fully revealed in these solitudes. For it lives all undisturbed, excepting by the man in waders. The birds flit about and around you without that kind of fear they exhibit in the open country, and the trout seem only to move away sufficiently to allow one to pass. The flash of the rod is only noticeable as part of the general flicker produced by the sun through the quivering leaves.

The man who loves our English river scenery, and does not feel fit enough to travel far in the open glare, should hie away to these unfrequented spots, when the foliage is full and the trout fat. If he can cast a flat line, here to the left, and there to the right, under the overhanging boughs, many a lusty trout will take, all unsuspectingly, his lure, and, in the quiet, as is invariably the way in Nature's deep retreats, life and death struggles will every now and then take place. But as soon as these are over, and before the thrilling sense of them has left the solitary fisherman, the pleasant murmur of the cascades will be heard again.

CHAPTER IX

MINNOW FISHING

EXCEPTING in the month of August and early September I seldom fish minnow, and, even then, my beats are kept strictly to water not usually fished with fly.

It is difficult to understand why, in these modern days of mechanically perfected spinning reels, some of the newer fishermen will persist in throwing a minnow at the very beginning of the season, when the water is at its prime for fly.

There are reaches in every river where large, cannibal trout are better taken out. It is in these that legitimate minnow fishing may conscientiously be pursued. I have discussed this question with experienced anglers, and river watchers who know what goes on in particular waters, and am convinced that judicious fishing with minnow, even in water otherwise reserved for fly, would occasionally, and at particular times in the season, serve a very useful purpose indeed.

H

On the Eamont and Eden large cannibal trout often leave Ullswater and go down-stream on murder bent. I have seen such ugly trout with hawk-like noses taken out with minnow.

A keeper told me last year that he had frequently seen big cannibal trout rush out of their lairs and seize smaller trout in thin water, of such a size that they could not be immediately swallowed, and that the brigand had to roll over and over with them down-stream until he was back in his hiding-place again.

In fishing of this kind I have confined myself to natural minnow. At the beginning of August I get a supply of these with a wire minnow-trap. Sometimes minnows are to be found in abundance in the river, but if I wish to make ready a good supply—a supply which will cover all the fishing I want to do—I take a day at one of the lakes where the minnows are more concentrated at particular spots.

The trap is baited with a few hard crumbs, or bits of dog biscuit, and let down at the end of a piece of rope into the water where the minnows assemble. Every now and then the trap is drawn up and emptied, and the middle-sized minnows, which are the best, sorted out, and the others thrown back. The selected minnows are laid between two rough towels to dry. When sufficient have been captured, and are fairly dry and dead, they are packed head to tail between layers of common salt, in old flat tobacco tins, like sardines. The drying does away to a great extent with the collection of brine in the boxes. They are examined next day, and if there is any brine it is allowed to trickle out.

In a briny box minnows are too soft for use. It is therefore advisable to see that the layers of salt are dry. The minnows will keep for three or four weeks in this way. But if it is desired to keep them longer in salt they should be bottled, and the cork sealed down.

Formalined minnows are not so good as those salted. The former probably smell, and are too stiff, but if soaked in fresh water for a short time before use some of the formalin smell is done away with. Salted minnows shrivel up a trifle but seem to retain their colour. They are, however, second rate to absolutely fresh caught minnows, and, when these latter can be procured as required, they are always to be preferred to any other. The day's supply can be put into a bottle of water where their flexibility and colour will be retained for that day.

As it is a bother to be always taking a minnow out of a bottle of water a few should be taken out at a time, and put into either an indiarubber sponge bag or tobacco pouch, where the moisture will be retained.

If an ordinary, stiffish, long rod is used, sufficient line is drawn off the reel into the left hand, and the cast shot through free-running rings, across and up-stream. The spin of the minnow is produced by drawing it through the water with several repeated sideway swings of the rod, partly across and against the current, the last, and often killing, movement being under the bank to the right of the fisherman.

This old-fashioned method of fishing the minnow had a good deal to be said for it. Between every swing-like draw of the rod there is a momentary stoppage, and following fish then often rush forward and seize their prey.

The modern spinning reel is dependent on the turn of the reel, and, although an expert can pro-duce some modification of the regular machine-like spin, he cannot humour it to best advantage as with the old, long rod.

The advantage of the modern spinning reel and short rod lies in the ease with which the minnow can be thrown out over a big area of water. But, having once started for the day with a short spin-ning rod, the sport is confined to what such a rod can do, and nothing else. A long general rod on the other hand allows of a change to " fly " whenever a suitable opportunity occurs. Therefore, to the young and energetic fisherman the more tiring but adaptable use of a long rod can be strongly recommended. The shorter rod and mechanical reel no doubt make their appeal on account of their ease to older fishermen.

This is the ease so far as I am concerned nowadays, and moreover I sometimes use a Malloch reel. It is the easiest spinning reel to cast with I have tried, and the disadvantage of kinking, which has been so much discussed lately, is readily cancelled by, now and again, taking off the cast, and allowing twenty or thirty yards of the line to recoil back again to their original straightness by flowing for a few minutes down-stream.

In throwing with a Malloch the automatic reaching forward of the left hand, at the finish of the cast, to grasp and turn the drum instantaneously is the most important feature of the whole business. At the same moment this left hand is in contact with the rod, and spinning with the right hand commences without any delay. A rod of this kind for trout fishing should be fairly supple, and allow of the use of fine gut traces and small hooks, so that, in its first striking shock it will not tear away the hold of the tackle from the jaws of the fish.

It has to be remembered that fish taking a

minnow are generally on the big side; that they rush at and seize it with a sudden, hefty pull or check, and in a very different way to fish taking a fly. These large fish capture minnows very much in the same way that a terrier catches a rabbit.

There is perhaps no better natural minnow tackle than that known as an " Ariel," but for spinning up-stream, in clear water, I have found that double hooks are less conspicuous than treble ones, and hold quite as well. In using the Ariel I always put on a small lead between the two swivels.

For coloured water minnow fishing, I have found nothing quite so economical or good as a crocodile tackle. It spins perfectly without the necessity of bending the minnow, and very frequently the same bait can be used again after taking off a trout.

I remember, on one occasion, when trout were evidently very busy with the Tommy Loaches after a flood, catching several trout with live loaches in their mouths. They dropped into my hand as I was releasing the tackle, and I straightway put them on to the Ariel and spared my own limited supply.

One old minnow fisherman who follows the fell becks, told me, some time ago, that he prefers a small bull-head to either a minnow or a loach. The latter and the bull-head, although not so silvery as minnows, are undoubtedly much tougher.

Beck fishing with minnow and a long rod will often, in August, afford a delightful day's sport. The minnow is thrown up the sides of the deep pools and streams, and dragged past the lairs under the banks. Very few beck fish can resist a bait of this kind as it spins past their peep holes.

CHAPTER X

THE FELL BECKS

A NORTHERN river like the Eden has to be considered in quite a different way from the slower running streams of the south. It is decidedly a mistake to conclude, at certain times in the season, that because the water in the main river is low and clear there is nothing to be done in the way of sport. Such a conclusion is altogether too conservative.

When the river is not fishing well, at certain off times, I have found it profitable, both from a sporting and a pleasure point of view, to turn to the becks.

There are fishermen who have gone to the Eden for years and yet know nothing whatever about the possibilities and charms of its tributary streams. On the other hand there are many good local fishermen who prefer the becks to the river, and seldom fish anything else.

Fishermen passing down the whole length of the

COLLEGE WATER, KIRKOSWALD, LOWER EDEN.

valley on the Midland Railway, from Wild Boar Fell to Carlisle, look out of the windows and see the Eden at its source, and occasionally farther down the valley where it has increased in size. In passing through the old Inglewood Forest district, between Lazonby and Carlisle, they catch glimpses of its most beautiful parts. It has then taken in the Eamont, and is a big, streamy river of great attraction.

These travellers, however, see nothing of the beck feeders, which have eaten their way deep down into the mountain gorges, and lower well-wooded ravines. Many anglers may be likened to travellers on main lines and great turnpikes. They miss, by their neglect of the becks, the less known, but frequently more beautiful, and at times profitable, by-ways of their sport. Their membership of some association, or tenancy of a famous river, ties them down to the beaten track.

In this connection it may be said that one has only to buy a motor-car to be condemned to follow the steam-roller. To have the keeper at your elbow is at best shared sport. Thoreau said he would " rather sit on a pumpkin and have it all to himself, than be crowded on a velvet cushion." And so it may be said of fell beck fishing, for it is better to leave your society behind you if you wish to realise, and enjoy, the stillness of the vast sombre chambers of the hills where rivers are born.

It is generally in July and August that fishermen who know turn their attention to the hill-burns, and do very well indeed on them. But I am not recommending them entirely on account of the baskets they provide. My chief point is that they do afford, besides sport, a really pleasant change, and take one away from the great and, as it were, dusty thoroughfares. Becks are not meant for great doings, but baskets are taken out of them that would compare favourably with those taken out of the river.

In considering the question of fishing these becks one of the chief points to be taken into account is the distance to be covered in the day. A reference to the sketch map provided will show the chief tributaries of the Upper and Lower Eden to Armathwaite. A fairly vigorous man could start at the bottom of any one of them and arrive well up into the hills by tea-time. But if less exertion is desired these becks can be split into halves, the Lower and the Upper, and the choice decided beforehand.

Waders are useful in the lower reaches, but not absolutely necessary, excepting in the Eamont.

If it is decided to go right up into the naked fell

gorges it is advisable to travel light, but not lighter than the weight of a substantial lunch. Short knee-top waders are useful all the way for crossing, but some fishermen only use a strong pair of shooting boots with nails.

In any case the start should be early, and the first cast be falling on the water not later than nine o'clock. Even when the intention is to set out and only fish lower reaches, one may often be tempted to go farther.

The rod should be of the general kind for casting either a fly or a worm, and at times a small minnow.

It is advisable, where possible, to keep well below the banks if wading. If not one should, at odd times, be prepared to creep on them. " Fine and far off " never appealed to me, but it is certainly sheer nonsense to use this method for becks. Here one cannot be far off, and to be fine is to be far too tender.

When your wild hill-burn trout is hooked he immediately makes violent efforts to get home under some old root, or hollow bank. Now a good deal has been written about " playing " trout, but I submit that in this case, the safest place is the pannier. It is well, too, to beware the conventional catch words, for quick despatch is the way of the

Wild. To put the matter in a nutshell one has to be undeniably masterful with beck trout.

The Alpha and Omega of beck fishing is, " Keep your scarecrow of a body out of sight! " The art of approach has as much to do with all kinds of clear water fishing as it has with golf and scouting, but once the lure of the hill-burns has got you good scouting will follow. I have often thought how amusing it would be for a hidden looker-on to watch a good beck fisherman in the lower reaches, dodging like a maniac from tree to tree, and from bank corner to bush, in the all-absorbing pursuit of his sport.

It is advisable to look well ahead if you do not know your water. Judicious crossing is necessary both for sport and legs. Always remembering that, other things being equal, the best bank is that facing the sun. But nearly every good rule has its important exception, and in this case it is when fishing coloured water.

It is to be hoped that the reader will not consider this rather special chapter too full of presumptuous " do's " and " don't's," for the writer has no desire to " lay down the law," or " point out royal roads."

The becks, in fact, give opportunity for research and experiment, and the more this attitude is taken be. In all kinds of sport it is a maddening and cramping job to try to remember the rules, and, even then, they may not suit you. The " do's " are done with, and the " don't's " have to follow, for what they are worth.

Don't try, in small becks, to see the lions feed. The inevitable penalty will be a light basket.

Don't set your feet down too heavily on those often hollow and vibrating banks. Fishermen shod with heavy brogues, or shooting boots, cannot be said to tread with fairy footsteps, but it is a desirable ideal to aim at on small streams.

Don't expect brown trout in fell becks to be lying out in full view in midstreams. If you do you will be apt to be disappointed, and hurt someone's feelings by saying there are no trout in them. It is not one of their daylight habits to be out of doors very much. They prefer to watch for their butcher and baker from behind the curtains of their little windows. When, however, they do see their daily bread coming down the street no one is kept waiting very long.

On all streams, be they large or small, there are particular runs known to acclimatised fishermen where sport can be relied upon. Very thin " all across kind of flat " water is generally barren. There is a national scarcity of under-bank cottages by the side of this kind of run. It is in the " trout villages " that you must hawk your bread, and at the odd " farmhouses " lying between.

Trout communities in becks are to be found where the banks run high and the bushes thick; behind boulders and big stones; at the foot of ancient walls; under old bridges, and round little corn mills.

Never on any account pass the noisy, gurgling " market " places, and, in choosing your beck itself, let your choice fall where there is plenty of splash. Fishing in " troubled waters " is not in this case unprofitable.

As you tread your way upwards through the lower, wooded reaches of the mountain homes of the brown trout, on a bright summer morning, you will hear the " gentle droning of the bees and the desultory twitter of birds." Getting farther and farther up your foot will, now and again, strike a musical limestone; and when you reach the bracken and heather the plaintive call of the curlew, the harsh croak of the raven, and the bleat of the mountain sheep, will tell you that you have reached a land where boundaries are unknown, and that you have passed out of the country of

"THE BIRTHPLACE OF A BECK," HIGH CUP NICK.

hedgerows and stone walls, and entered the great spaces.

If you have associated with Nature lovers like " Bob," a fresh chapter in your fishing life will have been opened, and you will want to read it again and again.

CHAPTER XI

GRAYLING FISHING IN THE EDEN

THOSE fishermen who are not content to leave the river after the trouting season is over may very well turn their attention to grayling fishing as a not unattractive sport.

It may appear on the face of it, from a weather point of view, a game only for the young and hardy, but this is not really the case. A long, hard day with these fish, excepting perhaps in the early autumn, when the weather conditions are often all that can be desired, is out of the question. The start need not be made before ten or eleven o'clock in the morning, and four or five hours' work is all that can be done.

Grayling feed in shoals. They are here to-day and perhaps somewhere else to-morrow, but the area of their habitual wandering is never very great. Certain suitable lengths of water carry plenty of fish, and when they are located there is no necessity for such hard, and long distance wading as is common in trout fishing. In regard to warmth in late autumn and deep winter, I have always found two pairs of stockings sufficient for the legs, and a thick woolly waistcoat for the body. But if there is a strong wind blowing the ordinary fishing jacket on the top keeps one snug and wind-proof. It is quite a mistake to put too much on. Sometimes I did this when I first started winter fishing, and found that I got too warm when walking.

The life history of the grayling in the Eden is comparatively short. They were put in as " fry " at Musgrave about the year 1880. I had an uncle living there then, and he had a good deal to do with it, although he protested to his friend, who was at the bottom of the business, that the river carried its full head of trout, and any competition in regard to the food supply would be injurious.

The tank of " fry " was tipped, by the old yeoman, into the river over the churchyard wall one night before a heavy flood. He was a keen trout fisherman, and was pleased to imagine that the interlopers would be washed down to the Solway.

I used to go and stay with him in those days, and we fished the river day and night; but, in his time, we never came across a grayling. He now sleeps peacefully under the sycamore trees, not far from where the tank was emptied, and, for all he knows, the Solway theory may have been correct.

In these days of the regular introduction of new species of fish into our sometimes depleted rivers it is well known that the fish themselves have the final word in the matter of a permanent home. If the new water suits their whim they stay, if not they mysteriously take themselves off like the Romans.

But the Upper Eden, with its fine, gravelly bottom, did suit the grayling, and they have grown and multiplied in that fourteen mile stretch of suitable water between Musgrave and the foot of the Eamont. Some odd ones are found below that limit, but the really good fishing is in the stretch mentioned. Although they are to be found at the mouths of tributary streams they seldom, if ever, run up them, and appear so far to shun the colder water, and rocky bottoms, of the Eamont and Lowther.

Grayling, as I have said, have a well-known habit of feeding in shoals, and the possibility of good sport depends largely upon locating them. From Musgrave to Ormside, however, one can hardly go wrong. But when you get farther down the river, below Temple Sowerby, where the water is bigger, the game of hide and seek is more pronounced, although the fish are still quite plentiful.

It is in October that fly fishing for grayling comes on. This remains good throughout the long fall of the leaf, in the pure air of Westmorland, and longer still if the winter, up to Christmas, is mild. The flies used should be small, and on this account the ordinary Eden trout flies sometimes answer the purpose quite well, and are generally adhered to by local anglers. Visitor grayling fishermen, however, use special flies, such as the Green Insect, Apple Green Dun, Red Tag, etc., following, in the main, Mr Pritt's example and teaching in this respect.

Sometimes it will be found that grayling hardly look at either the local or special flies. When the fall of the leaf is taking place it seems, at odd times, to bring on to the water some exasperating, minute insect, like the midge, on which the grayling feed all the time, just breaking the surface of the water with their noses, and paying scant attention to anything larger that is thrown over them.

Grayling are coming into season in late August and September, and, for an hour before darkness sets in, during these two months, good sport may be had with them at the tails of streams. Big baskets are often secured in the autumn with the fly. The sport is delightful in every way, and is practised in new colour surroundings, for the birch leaves are then of an ivory yellow, and the beeches a russet brown.

At Christmas time a very killing method of fishing for grayling is by the use of a small red worm, and frosty weather is the best for this purpose. A sprinkling of dry snow, and a fringing of the water with thin ice are sure harbingers of good sport. Wading for any length of time under such conditions is no doubt a cold job, but good sport can be had without wading at all.

This can be done by floating the worm down the stream below the fisherman provided with a rod with free running rings, an undressed silk line, and a reel with a free drum. The gut cast should be fine, but need not be more than four or five feet long. I prefer tackle made up with two of Hardy's No. 14 side-barbed hooks. They are marked " O " on page 153 of the latest catalogue. An easily adjustable float, made from a piece of cork, with a short peg—without rings run through it—to hold the line, is best.

Taking up a position at the head of a run, the float is fixed far enough above the bait to allow of it swimming down six or eight inches from the bottom in a medium depth of water. In deeper water it should be about half-way down, and, for both, shotted just sufficiently to "cock" the float. If wading it is desirable to get into the water at the top of the intended flow and fish down, paying the line out off the free drum in such a way that the float will not joggle. If the angler's sight is good he will be able to let it out below to the extent of twenty or thirty yards. As soon as the cork stops, or bobs, the moment has come to strike, off the reel.

The soft mouth of a grayling will not generally hold a "finger strike." At this time of the year, too, the grayling is a good fighter, and, when struck, his flashing body can often be seen in the bluish, winter water at the end of your line.

As opposed to wading, I know of places where fishing from the bank is quite practicable. One of these, for example, is on a gravel bed where two currents join, like the forks of the letter "Y." Standing in the angle, one throws down into the "Y" leg. The float is carried out at first by the strong current, but when it reaches the slowly moving water below the time for striking is at hand. If the fish are shoaled there you may continue to pull them out one after another until the end of the take.

Stormy weather is not as a rule good for grayling

fishing, but in times of flood, they seek quiet eddies under the banks, and take freely.

The undressed silk line should be well greased with mutton fat, and, if the weather is very frosty, occasionally rubbed down with a greasy rag. If this is not done, or even sometimes in spite of the precaution, the watery part of the line gets encrusted with particles of ice, which fill up, and make window panes of the rings, effectively stopping the line. The worms should, of course, be well cleaned in moss as already described, and ought not to be longer than about one-and-a-quarter inches, or even less.

Grayling are not so " pernickety " as is often imagined. It is altogether too limiting in practice to confine oneself to the laid down rules. The small worm mentioned covers a small tackle—that is all. Such a tackle, and fine gut, is necessary because the bait hangs down in full view. The grayling, however, do not object to a larger worm, on a larger tackle, when it is rolling down a stream, and does not appear to have a string attached to it.

There is plenty of room for experiment in this kind of fishing. The grayling is, however, a shy fish, and the art of keeping out of sight is a fixed necessary condition of the sport.

If a choice has to be made of time, there can be no doubt that fly fishing in the autumn stands pre-eminent. October in Westmorland is often a delightful month, and I at least like to tramp my way to the fishing through the woods of crackling, fallen leaves, to see the beeches and the bracken ablaze in sunlit brown, and, here and there, to pick off the bushes a ripe hazel nut.

The peewits and golden plover are at this time of the year gathered together in noisy circling crowds, and the gay tailed pheasants disappear under the bushes.

If the beginning of a trout fisherman's content is in the spring it may well be said that it has a glorious, and protracted ending in the autumn for the man who loves to throw a fly over both grayling and trout.

CHAPTER XII

THE ROUND OF THE SEASON

A NORTHERN river such as the Eden does not, as a general rule, begin to fish well before April. The trout are in poor condition in March, when the season first opens.

Wintry weather prevails in Westmorland and Cumberland from the beginning of November, but heavy snowstorms, and hard frosts, seldom occur before Christmas. It is after Christmas that the Pennine Fells are really stormbound, and covered with snow either right down to their feet, or along the whole length of their high tops.

The tributary becks of the Eden, which have their sources in the high mountain gorges, are not often actually frozen up, but their shallow edges are fringed with ice. The deep, lying snow melts slowly in the great hollows of the hills, and, excepting after heavy rains, only finds its way gradually into the becks, but for this reason it keeps them cold and clear far on into the month of April.

136

the shepherds begin to turn their flocks up into the walled-in pastures of the lower fell sides. They are chary of turning them right up on to the higher bleak tops too soon, for fear of losing them in the occasional late spring snowstorms.

The man who happens to have been born in a land of fells and mountain becks knows intuitively that the seasons of the shepherd run in parallel lines to those of the fisherman.

When the autumn days grow short and chill, and the trout begin to leave the Eden to go up the becks, the sheep begin to come down from the high pastures. When the days lengthen into spring the trout move down again with every little flood, and the old ewes of the sheep flocks, wintering in the valley, get restless, and long once more for their old haunts among the heather.

Landmarks stand out prominently in this valley of my story, and they are both weather breeders and weather tellers. It is customary there to associate places and conditions with one another: e.g., when the weather is bad in the early autumn the local people say, " It's Brough Hill weather." Brough Hill is the place of the great local horse fair held on the last day of September and the first day of October. After " Brough Hill " they expect nothing but cold and rain, snow and wild roaring winds, until March is out.

At the first bleating of the new born lambs, the spring-time of the trout fisherman's new season is at hand.

When with " Bob," I used to like to talk about all these changes; of the kind of flies we knew followed the disappearing snow, and the upward trend of the shepherd with his hardy, black-faced sheep. How the rising song of the birds was in tune with the time of the rising fish.

When the ash trees, so typical a feature of the pasture lands in the Eden Valley, are still bare at Whitsuntide it is said that the becks will be low.

To all country-born fishermen these nature-signs vary in interest. The day-time fisherman, for example, is far more interested in the early season signs than the night fisherman. He loves to see the wild celandine peeping out in the lanes, and to smell the budding larch: for they tell him plainly that the heyday of his sport is near, and that, soon, the still flabby trout will be strong enough to breast his favourite streams.

The night fisherman still bides his time. **The**

hawthorn is as yet too full of flower, and the peewits too concerned with family cares, for any near forecast of his particular pleasure. As soon, however, as the young birds begin to leave the nest, and the field mice roam nightly in the first real summer heat, the hoot of the brown owl tells him that his time, too, has come. These sounds are music to the ears of such " night birds " as the old Dicks of my " looking forward " days. Then it is that the great, fat, brown and white moths begin to flitter at twilight about the meadows by the riverside.

When the ash and the oak are fully dressed, and the great blaze of yellow gorse is fading away, the " bustard " carnival is in full swing. So the time of the still night fisherman comes " Just behind the sunshine and the song of the birds."

All through the month of June, perhaps the most glorious of all months in Westmorland, the devotees of the bustard ply their solitary craft. They wander off alone, just before darkness sets in, with " put up " rods and long shafted nets, to return in the small hours of the morning, as daylight slowly breaks, and the old villages still lie asleep under the fells.

When the cattle are to be seen sheltering under the trees from the heat of July and August suns, and the song of the birds has died down, fly fishermen of all kinds know that it is only for **one** odd hour out of the twenty-four that their tempting lures will be of any use—that magic hour just before dark.

It is in these seventh and eighth months of the year that the minnows begin to shoal in the quiet eddies, and the safe, thin water at the edges of the river. Their eyes are very quick, and sense of vibration keen. As you approach their retreats you must keep your shadow out of sight and set your feet down quietly—if you wish to watch them. For should you suddenly stand up you will not only see the minnows dash away, but odd trout also, which have been lurking on their borders. The reason for this is day-time-feeding trout follow the shoaling minnows in July and August.

It is at this time of the year that odd fishermen on the Eden begin to use the natural minnow as a bait, though not by any means all of them do it. The regular fly-man is seldom a minnow fisher. " Bob " used to speak of old Joe, and young so and so as " Minnow fishers "; distinguishing them from his own particular tribe in this way.

These minnow fishermen are not of the modern kind, fitted up with patent reels, who fish minnow at all times of the season and in all waters. Generally speaking, they only go out when the

THE SCAR, NEAR TEMPLE SOWERBY

water is right—a minnow water—copper coloured, and just falling after a flood.

The jack-of-all-trades is not common among fishermen. There are such men, but they are few and far between. So, on the Eden, one knows them by their real trades, as it were, distinctly and by reputation. Fly fishers; bustard fishers; creeper fishers; minnow fishers, and worm fishers.

In the holiday month of August visitor anglers regularly come to certain places on the Eden. It is surprising to notice how persistently they flog the gin-clear water day after day, and August after August. One imagines, that, this being the only time of the year during which they can fish, they must go away with the idea that there are few trout in the river. If, however, in this worst month of the season they could see the evening rise, just before dark, they would be reassured. It is a rise of some trout and many smolt.

It is not suggested that they would make great catches at this hour. Experienced fishers are then well content with a modest half-dozen. If you fish the main, open shallows, nearly every fish you hook will be an embryo salmon. The real, rising trout have to be sought for in other places; under the deep banks and overhanging trees.

If I wanted to whet the fly-fishing appetite of a

boy, and give him the sense of " rod touch," perhaps no better way could be devised than by putting him among the smolts on a midsummer evening. " Bob " always said that the delicate art of striking must come through having something to strike at.

When the hazel nuts are full, and the old women are gathering bramble berries in September, the trout are once more on the day-time feed. There is then, for a few weeks, a return on their part to spring ways both in regard to habitat and food.

September day-time fishing can be practised in the gently flowing flats, at the tails and heads of streams, and in the pools of the fell becks. Spring flies here come into service again.

Every little autumn flood beckons its quota of trout up to the old nurseries in the becks. Here the spawning grounds lie far away from the big river. I always think of these becks, when the bracken is turning yellow on their banks, as the safe refuge of motherhood. So far they are unpolluted. No chemical factories poison their waters. Innocent, old-world corn-mills still grind there as of yore. Rudyard Kipling calls attention to them in his inimitable way :

" See you the little mill that clacks,
    So busy by the brook?
She has ground her corn and paid her tax
    Ever since Domesday Book."

The banks skirting the lower parts of these breeding streams are often well wooded, and so overgrown that the possible, but improbable, netting poacher has no chance of wholesale success.

The grayling seldom go farther up the becks than a hundred yards from the mouth.   If, as some fishermen aver, these winter feeding fish play havoc with the ova of trout their depredations are confined to the Eden, where fewer trout spawn than in the becks.

In concluding this rambling chapter it may be said that, when the corn harvest has been gathered in, in late cropping Westmorland, and the stubble and turnips are still being shot over for partridge, grayling fishing begins.   It is the time of the fall of the leaf, beginning with the ash after the first frosty night, and ending in late November with the hard-leaved beech.

Then the season is over, and nothing further remains to be done but to foregather at night round the old firesides, to crack over the great days that have gone, and forecast hopefully those others still to come.

CHAPTER XIII

THE DIARY OF A WET FLY FISHER

FEW local fishermen on the Eden can spare time to take a full day with the rod. But, at the very beginning of the season, there are two days when they are off soon after nine o'clock in the morning, and these are Good Friday and Easter Monday.

Many of these fishermen are their own masters, in a small way, but have always their regular work to attend to. When fly fishing is at its best—from the middle of March to the end of May—they do contrive to take, now and then, a little extra time off. They are, of course, on the spot, and so can choose their days. Sometimes, when they have a few unexpected hours to spare, they may go out when the prospects of sport are none too good. Generally speaking, however, they carefully husband their leisure, and get well ahead beforehand with their work so that they may be able to take half a day when the signs are really propitious.

It goes without saying that such men are keen

anglers.   They started young, know their river, and dress their own flies accordingly.   No doubt, on many occasions, they feel greatly tempted to steal away when work demands their presence at home.   Men like " Bob," however, do not often neglect their real work for mere pleasure.   My experience of them is that the best workmen are generally the best fishermen.

The following diary may be both useful and interesting as being that of such a man, one who had to get away when best he could, and make the most of his odd times.   It will be seen that he started rather early in March and was fairly successful up to the 30th May.

I have extracted from his diary all the notes under the dates from 9th March to 30th May.

March 9.	14	trout	on	Light Snipe and Blue Hawk.
,, 14.	12	,,	,,	Light Snipe, Blue Hawk, Partridge and Orange, in a snowstorm.
,, 17.	20	,,	,,	Blue Hawk and Orange Partridge.
,, 24.	27	,, all on		Orange Partridge.
,, 28.	18	,,	on	Light Snipe and Orange Partridge.
April 1.	37	,,	,,	Light Snipe, Orange Partridge, Water-hen and Blue Hawk.

K

April 4.	27 trout on	Light Snipe, Blue Hawk and Orange Partridge.
,, 8.	32 ,, ,,	Light and Dark Snipe, Blue Hawk and Orange Partridge.
,, 11.	22 ,, ,,	Light Snipe and Water-hen.
,, 14.	24 ,, all on	Light Snipe.
,, 15.	12 ,, on	Light Snipe and Orange Partridge.
,, 18.	12 ,, ,,	Light Snipe and Water-hen.
,, 22.	16 ,, ,,	Light Woodcock, Light Snipe, and Water-hen.
,, 25.	17 ,, ,,	Light and Dark Snipe, and Water-hen.
,, 28.	16 ,, ,,	Dark Snipe, and Light Woodcock.
May 5.	20 ,, ,,	Dark Snipe, Light Woodcock and Water-hen.
,, 9.	50 ,, ,,	Light Woodcock, Dark Snipe, and Water-hen and Red.
,, 12.	14 ,, ,,	Light Woodcock, Water-hen, and Light Starling.
,, 16.	18 ,, ,,	Light Starling and Dark Snipe.
,, 21.	13 ,, ,,	Light Woodcock and Light Starling.
,, 23.	15 ,, ,,	Light Woodcock and Light Starling (at night).
,, 24.	6 ,, ,,	Light Woodcock and Light Starling (at night).
,, 30.	22 ,, ,,	Light Woodcock and Light Starling (at night).

An analysis of this diary shows the Light Snipe to have been the most killing fly up to the 25th April.

The Orange Partridge the next best up to the 15th April.

The Water-hen, tied with the Orange Partridge, but did not come into successful use until the 1st April.

The Blue Hawk came next, and was successful up to 8th April.

The Light Woodcock tied with the Blue Hawk, but did not come into use before 22nd April.

The Dark Snipe and Light Starling followed; the former coming into use for the first time on 8th April, and the latter, always a good late season day and night fly, not before 12th May.

I was surprised to see an entry, on 29th June, of trout being taken with the Blue Bottle. It shows to what straits the fly fisherman had been reduced for day-time fishing in the month of June, and also reminds me of something that would have otherwise slipped my memory—early dapping, or in the local dialect " Bobbing " days.

As a lad I often sallied forth with a long, light rod, and some blue bottle flies, to dap behind the trees. The Blue Bottle was impaled on a small No. 14 hook through the skin of the back, so that his legs

and wings were free and he remained alive. Only
a short length of fairly strong gut was used—not
more than half a yard. About six inches of line
were let out through the end ring of the rod.

After creeping up behind some big tree trunk or
thick bush the rod-point was stealthily pushed
forward over the deep water, until a trout
was seen to pass underneath. As soon as he
passed, up or down, on his chosen short beat, the
fly was lowered on to the surface of the water. It
looked lively and tempting enough when its legs
dangled and quivered there. The trout by this
time had turned, and, spying the newly fallen blue
bottle, generally made straight for it, coming up
to its prey from directly below, never sideways.

From one's place of concealment every movement of the fish could be clearly seen, and as, with
wide-open mouth, it appeared to have got the fly,
one struck, but generally far too soon. The trout
would have a puzzled look in its great eyes as it
turned down again, for it had not been touched,
and the fly was probably fast into a low branch of
an overhanging tree !

The art of dapping—keeping quite still and out
of sight—was, however, soon acquired, and, when
trout opened their mouths immediately under the
fly, the rod-point was gently lowered to allow the

lure to be properly sucked down and in. Then successful striking immediately took place, and short shrift was given to the fly-catcher.

Other flies beside blue bottles were used, and the best of these were the large stone flies. No prowling, under-tree trout could resist this last big morsel. We used also to dap deep with caddis worms and wasp grub; but I merely mention these side issues as part of the general apprenticeship to fishing, and as the result of this unusual entry in the diary.

Between the end of May and the beginning of September there are few noteworthy entries in the diary. In September fair catches of trout are again recorded; all on spring flies. There are notes also of grayling caught with such flies as Light Woodcock, Water-hen, and Light Starling, up to the end of October.

No special grayling flies are mentioned, but some few local anglers on the Eden do use the Red Tag in addition to the flies named above.

The diarist is an old friend of my boyhood days, as good a fisherman as " Bob," but more dour and solitary in his habits. He cannot be said to be secretive like old Dick, but, like many sterling men of the north country, he is not given to the wasting of words. Types like " Bob " are less common.

Besides the possession of great practical skill gradually acquired from youth upwards, they carry with them a kind of magic of the becks. There was also, and always, in " Bob " an undefinable music of the soul which harmonised with the splash of water and the song of the birds.

Perhaps these characteristics may be best described as the outcome of a keen and inborn sense of environment.

The allurement of fishing to such a man was not of the basket alone, but of the great wild.

As " Bob's " apprentices grew up, and some few of them went forth into the great world, far away from the quiet valley of the Eden, they became more and more conscious of his charm. They knew that he carried with him the secret of the river. Perhaps, too, as the years rolled by, there did come to some few of his disciples something of the real soul of the Eden's music and pastoral beauty.

SUPPLEMENTARY   NOTES

THE EDEN AS A TROUTING RIVER

Mr Marston, the well-known editor of the *Fishing Gazette*, has said that if the netting of freshwater fish could be prohibited the Eden would soon become one of the best fishing rivers in the country, and, as though in reply to this opinion, the River Eden Fishery Board have just recently issued such a prohibition. It reads as follows:

RIVER EDEN FISHERY DISTRICT

NEW BY-LAWS

(Certificate dated Sept. 24th, 1921.)

" Within that part of the Eden Fishery District which lies above the church at Grimsdale in Eden, the use of any net for taking freshwater fish, other than a fixed net for eels, a casting or dip net lawfully used for taking bait, or a landing net used as auxiliary to angling with rod and line is hereby prohibited.

" Provided that this by-law shall not apply to the use of a net under and in accordance with the conditions of a written permission of the Fishery Board, signed by the Chairman or Clerk of the Board, which permission shall only be granted for the purpose of facilitating the destruction or removal of Pike or other fish injurious to the salmon and trout fisheries.

" Any person using a net in contravention of this by-law shall be liable for each offence to a penalty not exceeding £5 and to the seizure and on summary conviction to the forfeiture of such net, and of all fish found in his possession or caught by such net.

" (*Signed*) FRANCIS W. SOAL,

" (*Clerk to the Fishery Board*)."

The whole of the Eden, with its tributary streams, runs through a pastoral country. There are no polluting factories on its banks, and it is fed from the great, upland pastures, and high fells, by mountain becks that never run dry. Its waters are so pure that they can be drunk without fear. The becks tumble down from the fells, and empty themselves into the river, in a perfect state of aeration. The big streams of the Eden rush along their course only to be held up momentarily by the occasional deep flats.

The Upper Eden, above the Eamont, runs off limestone, and soft red sandstone, over a gravelly bottom. The Lower Eden, below the Eamont, is strikingly different from the Upper Eden, for it is much more stony. It becomes a big river from this point, running mainly through densely timbered country, and, at times, through beautifully wooded, red sandstone gorges. That section throughout its

THE EDEN BELOW LANGWATHY BRIDGE.

(From a painting by G. O. Owen.)

length from Kirkoswald to Wetherall is perhaps unsurpassed in this country for perfection of river scenery.

All the way from its source at the top of the dale of Mallerstang down to Carlisle, where it becomes tidal, it passes through no large towns. Appleby and Kirkby Stephen, the two largest places on its non-tidal banks, are but small market towns of some two or three thousand inhabitants. None of the few farming villages on its banks reach a population of over two or three hundred people, and, in spite of any netting that has been carried on by licence, the Eden has always borne a good stock of trout.

The spawning grounds in the fell becks are ideal in every way. Fish food of all kinds is abundant, and includes besides minnows, leeches and bull-heads, a wide range of aquatic insects.

There are pike in some of the deep pools of the Lower, but none in the Upper, Eden.

Grayling were put into the river at Musgrave about forty years ago, and have thriven and multi-plied at such a rate, in the too kind waters of the Upper Eden, that the charge brought against them of abusing hospitality cannot be said to be unfair.

There are chub in some of the deep flats.

Pike, chub, and grayling all come under that

part of the new by-law which allows of netting for the purpose of facilitating the destruction of fish injurious to the salmon and trout fisheries.

Pike and chub are always dealt with unmercifully, if not sufficiently methodically. Grayling are looked upon, at any rate on the Upper Eden, with more favour. In their season, from August to February, they provide both good sport and food.

The question in regard to grayling is as to the extent to which they deplete the number of trout by competition in the available food supply, and by depredations into the spawning beds of the trout. There can be no doubt that they consume a big share of the food supply of the river, and, on this account, are serious competitors with the trout. Rigorous netting is therefore desirable.

The possible harm that grayling may do in raiding the spawning beds of the trout is altogether a more doubtful question. Grayling do not, as a general rule, run up the fell becks. On the other hand Eden trout spawn chiefly in the high tributary streams. Spawning trout run up the becks with the first autumn floods, and remain there until the early Spring. There is a good deal to be said for the local opinion that trout, being on the spot at the right time, are likely to play greater havoc with the grayling ova than the grayling can possibly do with the trout ova.

Of all the trouting streams in the Eden valley the Eamont, and particularly the lower reaches from Brougham Castle to Edenhall, carries the largest amount of fish food.   Its stock of trout is also good, but might be much greater.   I have examined the bottom and edges of this delightful tributary at all seasons of the year.   A stone cannot be lifted, and it is very stony, or a weed bed disturbed without a superabundance of aquatic life being revealed.

Many of the quiet backwaters have their bottoms covered with stick caddis.   The stone housed caddis are also plentiful.   All the way up, by the famous red sandstone caves of primitive man, virgin forest overhangs the river and scatters all kinds of landborn insects into the bluish lake-born water.

But the Eamont is also a safe refuge to many of the natural enemies of trout.

Not far from its woody banks there exists the large and ancient heronry of the Musgraves at Edenhall.   The herons have their nests in the great gaunt Scotch firs that surround the north end of Edenhall Lake.   I have sometimes been on the lake at breeding time, when the young herons are crowding the nests, and, sitting quietly in the boat, I have watched the parent birds feeding their ravenous young. They were continuously on the wing, to and from the river, all night long. The otherwise still night was consequently broken by an incessant squawking, like nothing so much as the barking of a big kennel of hoarse-throated dogs. One disturbs odd, fishing herons, in broad daylight both on the Eden and Eamont, but as darkness sets in their main feeding time begins.

If out early in the morning one will disturb numbers of them, still at their unfinished night task.

The Lower Eamont is also the so far safe home of otters. The great crevices in many of the rocks afford safe harbourage from hounds, and the only way to lessen their number seems to be by trapping.

Kingfishers and Water Ouzels are numerous on this stream, and on many of the tributary becks of the Eden. The Lyvennet, which enters the Eden at Temple Sowerby, is the beck to which I would take a naturalist to see kingfishers. These natural enemies of the trout are altogether delightful objects in themselves, and have added greatly to the charm of my fishing. I could not possibly bring myself to the point of shooting any of them, and, indeed, only suggest trapping in connection with the otters as a method of keeping them within reasonable bounds.

There is no need on the Eden, provided as it **is**

with such good natural spawning grounds in the becks, for artificial stocking, and more especially were the grayling, herons, and otters thinned out regularly.

The heronry was at one time much larger than it is now, and situated nearer the family seat of Sir Richard Musgrave, and close to it was one of the largest rookeries in the north of England. Some twenty years ago war broke out between the herons and rooks, and the fight for mastery raged for several days. The scene of this strange battle was the great park round the mansion. Dead combatants from both sides strewed the ground under the trees; but despite the fact that more rooks than herons were numbered amongst the slain the latter were defeated by force of numbers, and driven out of the park to the wood bordering the lake.

THE INSECT FOOD OF TROUT

I AM indebted to an entomological authority, and fishing friend, for the following notes on some of the aquatic animal life he has found in the Eden and its tributary streams.

Small dragon-flies of the Agrion species.

Duns of the Baetis species; abundant beneath the stones of streams.

Several species of Caddis-fly larvæ, which the trout apparently take case and all. They are as follows:—

Stenophylax, Micropterna, Halesus, Sericostoma and Plectronemia species. These all have cases of small stones. Caddis-fly cases are frequently found in fish that have just been caught.

There are a number of beetle larvæ, which fall victims to the trout. Two or three species of Agabus breed freely, many Hydropori, several species of Haliplus, two species of Deronectus, and one of the very abundant but seldom seen species of Whirligig beetle, Orectochilus Villosis.   This latter beetle is nocturnal.   My friend says that he has often thought, on quiet summer evenings, when he could hear fish sucking something in preference to his fly, that it was this beetle which attracted them.

Several species of Helephorus are abundant, and no doubt form a constant food supply in the neighbourhood of water vegetation.

The larvæ of the Alder Fly (Sialis) abound.

Many species of Chironomidæ and Tanyphus are plentiful in the mud and on plants.

The larvæ of the Sand Fly (Simulium) is plentiful in the shallow streams of both the river, and becks, where the water is constantly on the move over beds of weeds.

In all the streamy parts of the river, and becks, the larvæ of the Stone-fly (Perla) is grossly abundant, and provides, during April and May, an enormous supply of rich food.

THE INTELLIGENCE OF TROUT

FISHERMEN often wonder where instinct in trout ends and a form of reasoning begins. In this respect trout can be said to be quite different from insects, which are guided in life purely by instinct. There can be no doubt that experience plays an important part in the lives of trout. A pricked trout is much more shy than an unpricked one. " Once bitten twice shy " is, no doubt, true in regard to some of their experiences.

Individual trout certainly do get to know that man is a dangerous animal. They have seen dreadful things happen in his presence. He is quite different from all other animals frequenting the banks of rivers, for he stands upright, and waves his arms about. No other animal does this.

Occasionally violently struggling trout are to be seen being dragged towards him by invisible and mysterious means. It is quite clear that adult trout in fishing rivers soon become suspicious and wary in the known presence of man. The sight of man is always a warning signal. If he can fish without being seen the greatest obstacle, perhaps, to success has been overcome.

Trout associate man with the mysterious. Mystery alarms all the children of the wild. Trout rise continuously quite near, and all around, the night fisherman. Neither his body nor his arm movements are taken any notice of for the simple reason that they are not seen.

They know by experience that the natural fly food on which they live has a steadfast behaviour of its own. It does not float up or across stream. Natural flies are not attached to one another by pieces of string. Looked up at from below, towards the light of day, insect food on the surface of the water is more or less transparent. The unusual arouses suspicion. Natural flies have no solid vertebræ. The steel hook, running through the middle of an artificial fly is impenetrable to light. It is indispensable but, nevertheless, at times, an undoubted danger signal.

Nearly all wild things take care intelligently. Young animal life is subject to many blunders through inexperience. Self protection is instinctive from the first. It is afterwards reinforced by experience.

Fish do not stand high in comparison with other animals in intelligence. Life under water is not conducive to the growth of great intelligence. The environment of freshwater fish is very restricted. Except in regard to competition for food there is little of a stimulative character in their lives. The great and enlivening sense of hearing is absent. The sight of fish is set in a fixed stare. It does not change its direction or dimensions, and is unaccommodating in regard to the judgment of distance. The sole overpowering motive of life is feeding.

The sense of smell cannot be so highly developed in fish as in animals breathing free air. Fish eat what they have found to be satisfying and harmless. The young fry are not schooled or nourished by their parents. They have to fend for, and take care of, themselves. The number of trout that survive infancy is probably infinitesimal compared with the vast numbers that are eaten up by adult fish, herons, kingfishers, etc.

4

THE SIGHT AND HEARING OF TROUT

OCCASIONALLY " Bob " would talk to his little band of followers about the peculiarities of trout. He never talked to us of set purpose, and as the paid teacher, and it was always some boyish argument, or odd remark, that set him going. The little things that were constantly happening at the riverside provided us with a kind of jungle lore. The things he said to us would probably not have been said to grown men. He had a sense of his own simplicity of outlook, and knew that we should always listen in an understanding way.

The grown man, whose surmises had developed into conviction, retained, in spite of years, the freshness and wonder of boys, and a book could be written on the enthralling conversations that took place between us.

Perhaps we might have a freshly caught trout lying, sparkling on the grass—to us the most beautiful thing in creation—when some allusion

165

would be made to a striking characteristic such as the great, motionless eyes. The intensity of boyish curiosity always pleased " Bob," and drew him into our little group. " Aye," he would say, in the broad Westmorland dialect that fitted his musical voice so well, " troot nivver ga to sleep or shut their ees. They haven't any eyelids like ye blinken lads. They've ees summat like Jim Southard's. Jim's stiddy, wide oppen stare allus reminds me o' fishes ees. They nivver wink, nea, not in t' breetest sunleet. Ye can't tell what they're thinken about from their ees; whether they're pleased wi' what yer showen them or not. When ye'v gitten them oot o' t' watter the glassy stare doesn't change."

We were sometimes a noisy crew, and often wondered whether the fish could hear us laughing and talking. If they happened, occasionally, to be particularly shy we became fearful that they were being scared by the noise of our voices, and used to tell one another to " shut up." Then " Bob " would, as likely as not, step in. " Hear! they've laal use for hearing in t' watter. It's varra quiet doon below where they live. Ye can depend on't if they could hear they'd hev concerts in t' spring like t' birds. They're as happy in ther oan quiet way as t' larks when t' winter's ower. Nay, nay, ye needn't worry aboot t' noise ye mak; they can naither hear nor speak. Things that hear can generally say summat. Ye cannot be oot in t' fields and t' woods withoot knowen that. Talken and singen's varra smittal (infectious). It aw comes fra what t' scheulmaister used to caw imitation, but what ah caw followen yan another. T' poor troot cannot gie mooth to their pleasures. Tom Sarginson's like t' troot. He was boorn that way withoot any hearing; but if ye knock hard eneugh at his oald dooer, or walk across his loft, he knows yer aboot withoot seeing ye. Ye'll remimber what ahve often said aboot clampen yer feet on t' banks. That's just like walken on Tom's loft and tells t' fish yer comen as weel as words. Another thing ye'll hev to be careful aboot is rattlen t' big stanes togither when yer in t' watter. T' troot el know as weel as Tom, that yer comen, if ye dea that. Ahve hard it said, that there is a bit of an oald time ear inside o' t' heed o' fish and that it's likely they could hear yance on a time, but it's ower far back for us to havver aboot."

We used also to ask why we seemed to hook more fish on a sunk than a floating fly.

" Troot git hoald o' things below t' surface better than on t' top. They're not varra good judges o' distance. In some kinds o' leet they score a lot o' misses for ya bullseye. When they're moven aboot just below t' top they seem to be surer, but when they hev to come up a bit to a floaten flee they're not so sure o' their aim. Ah often think they want to git near eneugh to feel t' flee. Ye mebbe don't know that troot feel wi' their lips. It's t' standen flee that bothers them. A hauf drooned flee they git t' first try. Leet hes a lot to dea wi' fishin. It sometimes bothers t' seet o' t' fish and generally alters t' leuk o' flees. Ah often think t' fish are like cats. They seem to see best in t' dark."

He would also say, " Noo, if t't troot are not troubled much wi' what other folk are talken aboot they'll varra likely be minden ther own business. They've nobbet ya traide and that's t' provision traide. Nowt else matters to them withoot it's t' seet o' some o' ye on t' bank or an otter in t' beck."

We used to catch flies and show them to " Bob." Questions of colour and legs, etc., used to come up. He would say, in relation to the outstanding or distinguishing feature of these insects, " Aye, aye, they've six legs reet eneugh but ah don't think t' troot ivver trouble to count them before breakfast."

Then his leading principle in regard to fly making would come out. " It's t' shaddo of a flee ye catch fish wi'." This idea of a ghostly looking fly, a kind of apparition, was ever present with " Bob." His creations in the way of flies were made to meet this end, and of the softest feathers. Sharp outline and bushy substance **was** avoided, but truth to natural shape and size striven for and found. The dressing was certainly of that gauzy, to-**be**-seen-through kind, which is associated with spectres.

HABITAT OF AQUATIC INSECTS

It is in the shallow warmer water that much of the insect food of fish must be looked for. Water that has been said to be richer in living things than in any other element of the earth's surface. In it grows that plant life to which many of the aquatic tribe cling, and hide from their enemies.

But the different orders of aquatic animal life have their own particular likes and dislikes in regard to habitat. For example it is not in shallow fresh water that you must expect to find the mutitudinous gnats, but in the muddy, ditchy places where vegetable life is rank, and the green top-growth covers up a dense undergrowth of decay.

For the Perla nymph it is necessary to wade into the middle of stony, turbulent streams, and for the stone-fly to search the often still more stony, dry, gravel beds.

THE APPEARANCE OF FLIES, ETC.

In the sober colouring of the typical, and regular fly food of trout, there is something of that which is known as obliterative colouring. Sharp contrasts in colour are not common in these insects. The tell-tale effect of light and shade is neutralised.

Seen from below, on the surface film of the water, insects certainly show very little of the colour which is to be seen when they are laid out on a sheet of paper. They probably only appear to the trout as ghostly images of flies. Except from an advantageous position on the part of the trout immediately below the fly, they will not readily be seen at all. When trout are " on the feed," and near the top of the water, natural flies are more easily seen, and artificial flies much more readily taken. A fly making a great fuss to get off the water, immediately attracts attention, and may bring trout up from a greater depth of water. Movement is undoubtedly the great revealer. A perfectly still object may float quietly on the surface of the water without attracting particular attention. Immediately it moves, or turns, or flutters, however, parts of it will catch the light and affect the eye of fish watching from below, or, at certain angles, from the side.

Some of the landborn flies dislike water, and also some of the aquatic ones, like the Great Perla, for example. They make violent efforts to get away from it, and attract immediate attention. Many of the aquatic insects after reaching the top of the water, sail along as if asleep, and unconscious of any lurking enemy. These latter are the creatures, coming into the range of vision of the trout, that appear as blurred silhouettes on the surface of the water. They represent the shape of a fly without much colour except such as may be reflected from the bottom of the river. A natural fly alighting or being blown on to the water, retains some kind of tell-tale movement up to the moment of alighting. Trout catch some ray of light given off at that moment, and rise up to examine or take the fly. If the fly is now quite still, the revealing glint of movement has been quite enough to bring it under inspection, and it may then be taken. If there is what is known as a big hatch of flies on the water, trout come " on the feed," and are nearer the surface, where they can detect the flies in spite of the absence of movement.

The pupæ of insects rising to the surface of the water at the time of metamorphosis are sometimes fed upon by trout before they reach the surface. The principle of movement must play a large part in betrayal here.

Insects that have undergone complete metamorphosis are regularly fed upon by trout under the surface. Besides shape and movement, colour comes into play here. A sunk, wet, artificial fly is often much more killing than a floating fly. The sight, and judgment of distance, of trout, is probably better in regard to objects under the water, than motionless ones standing on the surface film.

Wet fly fishermen will probably generally agree that a yellow-bodied artificial fly accounts for many of their best baskets. This colour of body is well adapted to catch glints of light. In this connection, it is interesting to consider the nymph of the Stone-fly (Perla), known to anglers as the creeper. The sight of man is generally acknowledged to be quite as good as that of trout, yet it is extremely difficult for him to see a creeper on the bottom of a stream, so perfect is the protective colouring of its back. As soon, however, as it is disturbed and loses its feet, the glint of its yellow body betrays it.

Besides the glinting body of an artificial wet fly, the softness and wavyness of the hackle and wings is of the utmost importance. If the feathers are not soft, or are bunched together in too great a mass, their movement will be decreased, and their power of attraction, to say the least, considerably minimised.

In glaring sunlight, reflection from the river's bottom must play a large part in regard to the modification of colour tone.

It is a moot question how much the natural transparency of insects is revealed when looked at from below towards the light. The body and wings of flies, however, leaving out altogether the question of colour, must reveal something of natural size and form. Size, form, and movement are, therefore, very important considerations for the fly dresser.

Fishermen like " Bob " know this from long experience—from both failure and success. They frequently catch flies and examine them for this very purpose.

The hinge on which the more common actions of trout turn is the food question.

I remember many years ago rummaging through an old gun-box in which an aged fishing relative at Musgrave, on the Eden, kept his flies. We were going out to fish. Just before starting the old man selected a few flies from the box. The moths had played sad havoc with the wings. On my drawing attention to this he at once said, " It's the body that matters not the wings." He was a very successful fisherman. There is something in what he said, and I have never forgotten it. Nevertheless, hackle and wings have a good deal to do with form, and cannot be disregarded. I have no doubt, however, that the old man's ragged-looking flies would generally account for more fish than some of the bushy varieties one comes across.

Gaudy coloured flies, particularly of the ringed pattern, are danger signals to trout. The gay livery of the common wasp, for example, soon becomes known and respected—at a distance.

Insects of the wasp order are coloured to be seen not hidden. Both the under and upper surfaces of their bodies show sharp contrasts of colour. Even in reflected light from the bottom of the river the distinct pattern cannot but be seen. Such colours are quite different from those of harmless, edible flies, for they are much cruder, and more strikingly contrasted.

Besides those members of the Hymenoptera family that are hurtful and unpalatable, there are other members, which although coloured and ringed in a mimicking, waspish way, are mere frauds.

They only look dangerous.   Trout even get to know this characteristic at times.

Saw-flies, for example, are often blown on to the river in large numbers from willowy banks in summer-time.   They make violent efforts to get off again.   This sort of commotion rouses the trout. After cautiously trying a few of them, without suffering any inconvenience, they indulge in a good feed.   A " partridge and orange " comes in very well at such odd times as these; for although this artificial is not ringed it has a suitable body, and conforms well to size.   It is, in fact, a first rate ghost of the real thing.

INSECTS have six legs on which they stand with extraordinary firmness. The tense surface film of pools and flat gliding water supports them like a plank. Stone-flies glide over the surface of flat water as if they were skating. Some insects have only two wings, but the majority have four. The power of flight is their great asset. It enables them to change their quarters, and choose suitable homes.

Although insects have no internal skeleton they have remarkably hard skins. They are also a distinctly hairy race. The colour and obliterative protective colouring is frequently determined by their hairs.

Maimed and headless insects can frequently walk, and even fly, for hours after mutilation. This characteristic is very interesting to anglers, who often see them dashed by strong winds against trees, and the hard banks of rivers. It is something to remember that parts of them will most likely be alive after the roughest treatment, and continue that muscular action so attractive to the keen eyes of feeding trout.

Insects respond, according to their particular stimuli, to variations of wind, light, heat and cold. Their behaviour depends upon these responses, which are instinctive, and have nothing to do with consciousness or experience.

THE LOCAL ANGLER

THE geographical stronghold—that is the faith of the local angler—is generally built on some kind of solid and reliable foundation. It may have an ancient look about it, and require judicious patching here and there, but its preservation counts for more with some of us than a whole row of new houses.

  " Bob's " art of fly dressing did not show a knowledge of entomological facts, it must, therefore, be that his own personal sense of the appearance of flies did so. Probably at the back of his mind there was the idea that the trout saw them more in his way than in the microscopical way of the student of natural history. He was not only a keen observer, but a fixed one. His apprentices knew that he was invested with previous knowledge, and could lead them to places where things could be found. He was full of charity, but apt to look

askance at the man who frightened the fish away by
two great a show of entomological knowledge at the
end of his cast.   He classified his insects according
to the times of their coming on to the water, their
stay, behaviour, habitat, and appearance to the eye.
Generic and specific names did not trouble him in
the least.

It has been far too customary to describe fishermen of the local type as blind followers of a
" chuck and chance it " method.   By inference
some writers have set them down merely as winners
by accident—" flukists."   There is certainly a naïve
kind of simplicity about their sport which some
cocksure men might easily take for ignorance.   If
it had been at all possible to turn a nature-lover
like " Bob " away from himself into the realm of the
didactic, and doctrinal, in fishing his imagination
and sense of the river must surely have perished.
Then he would not have been the lodestone, the
native magnet, which drew together the school round
the old kitchen hearth.   He would have been a
second Squeers, and the mental growth of his pupils
would have been retarded, and perhaps entirely
stopped, by hunger of the soul.

The best type of local angler does not fake
his flies.   He uses his feathers with the utmost
simplicity and economy.   There is great restraint

in all his "dressings." His wizardry, which has been called luck, has nothing of the heroic about it. If he was a mere pot-boiler he would not be above looking for all the wonderful inventions that are said to " kill " in spite of folly.

THE SAVING GRACE OF FISHING

THE writer, as a loyal apprentice of " Bob," cannot help but think of boys. He has boys of his own. The hobby of fishing provides against loafing—against what is known at certain times as being at a dangerous " loose end." It is healthy—it creates a motive for thought. " Mens sana in corpore sano," can with confidence be emblazoned on its shield.

The idea that it is worth while to nurse the young sportsman has something to do, in this book, with the extolling of a particular type of fishing father. The different local " Bob's " that are by nature cut out to inspire boys are men of broad sympathy. They are permeated with wise tradition, full of knowledge, shy of mere precept, teachers by example, never in a hurry with spontaneous youth. A great churchman, who knew boys, once addressed some words to Father Time, beseeching him not to hurry with the boys.

182

NUNNERY WATER, LOWER EDEN.

" Let them be a little space,
  Tho' they lack our crowning grace;
  Tho' their talk be not about
  Things we talk of, dining out;
  Tho' their jokes are hard to see;
  Let them be.

  Could we once have been as they?
  Fat and rosy, fresh and gay,
  With such reverence for the fact,
  With such perfect want of tact,
  Yes? Well, all the same, prithee
  Let them be."

TACKLE AND THE MAN

A NORTHERN fisherman friend, who is also a first-rate shot, went out last year with two novices. They had taken the shoot but could not get a bird. My friend maintained there were plenty of birds. So they sallied forth together, and he proceeded to knock down one bird after another, until one of his companions asked him, " Where did you get that gun? "

" At Penrith for ten pounds," was the answer.

" Ten pounds! " said the over-dressed novice, " why I gave a hundred pounds for mine."

" Aye, aye," said my friend, " but it's not the gun, it's the man."

It is much the same with fishing. In spite of all the new inventions, expensive rods and tackle, over-dressed and gaudy looking flies, it eventually filters down to this great principle, as in all sport, it's the man that matters, and not his rig-out.

RODS AND TACKLE

A GOOD rod must always stand out as the most important and significant thing in fishing gear.

Men take particular care of their favourite rods. The beginner's first rod marks him down as a fisherman. Any disaster that happens to it is heart-rending. Woe betide any other boy who unluckily steps upon it. But although it is this kind of treasure, and a possession beyond all price, it need not at that time be expensive. It really only seems to be " The Rod." The right rod follows the time marking the sense of touch and rhythm, and has to be " found."

Fortunately this country is unexcelled in the rod making business, and when the beginner has finally made up his mind as to his needs in respect of weight, strength, and length, he can do no better than go to one of the several, good makers. He can, of course, without much trouble, choose from the catalogues, some one of the well-known and specially named standardised rods, and order it by post, or over the counter.

It is, however, much easier to order what is wanted than to get it.   The best method really is to " find " your right rod.   Study the catalogued specifications, then go and actually handle the particular kinds you think ought to suit you, not in the shop but outside, and with a reel and line on them.

Patience is indeed a great virtue in the matter of rod choosing.   Its exercise will often save a deal of unnecessary expense.   Nearly all seasoned fishermen will tell you that they spent a lot of money before they discovered their " answering " fly rod. The number of discarded, expensive rods hanging in fishermen's cupboards must be legion.   These do not quite suit their owners, but might exactly suit someone else.   Suitable rods are sometimes luckily picked up on this account.   It is very much the same with golf clubs; the prizes are generally picked up at odd times, and seldom by ordering.

True rod rhythm goes with the individual.   The right rod can be used without apparent effort.   I am simply speaking from experience, and have no desire to make any positive assertions in connection with what must always be, to a large extent, a matter of personal feeling.   Subject to this proviso I should say that, although lightness in a fly **rod** generally counts for ease, it should not be too light to throw a good standard fly line such as the Corona.

A line that can be cast into the teeth of a strong wind is not light. Therefore the rod should be heavy enough to carry it. The reel and line should balance the otherwise perfect, but naked, rod. Too light a reel will make the rod feel top heavy. On the other hand, if there is too much weight in the reel for the rod the hand will not be in feeling touch with the top. The reel and line clothe the bare rod, but are more important in regard to satisfactory fit, from a fishing point of view, than the clothes of the fishermen.

Some men find that a good second half of their fishing joy lies in making their own rods and tackle. Since the making of my first rod, already mentioned, I have made a round dozen. They were round enough, and gave me no end of pleasure— in the making. The regular rod makers, however, beat the amateur every time. Their rods are built to an exquisite perfection, and are models of skilled craftsmanship.

Nets, panniers, casts, tackle, flies, all come, however, more within the realm of amateur ability than rods. The various parts are easily obtained.

Their assembly is not a difficult matter, and gives scope for the exercise of individuality.

The satisfaction found in making my own nets and panniers has not been confined merely to the pleasure of making. Friends have admired them, and work without profit has been plentiful, and with much satisfaction to the soul.

Once I started on the great adventure of making a pair of brogues. My idea was to depart from the style of the shops and have wooden soles, broad and light, and good. Alas, they became clogged up with snow on their very first outing to the river, and, like the rods, never again saw the light of an uncertain northern spring day.

Minnow, creeper, stone-fly, and worming tackles are all easy to make. The tying on of hooks, in such-like operations, leads up to the finer art of fly tying. " Bob's " apprentices learned how to attach gut to shanked hooks long before touching a fly. Neat and secure tying comes by practice. In those days of long ago eyed hooks were unknown. Everything had to be tied, splices of rods, rings, nets, hooks, and all the various bait tackles. We were like sailors, never at a loss when tackle was broken. Mending the damage carried with it the satisfactory feeling of self-reliance.

There is such a thing as becoming attuned to the

many-sidedness of a hobby like fishing. One cannot become altogether accordant with such a great pastime unless able to do most of the things for yourself.

Of all the fishing gear that a beginner should learn to make artificial flies stand first in importance.

It is the study of the live insect in its natural habitat, for the purpose of fishing, that raises the sport of angling on to its high plane of intelligent endeavour.

The young enthusiast will be well advised to set about dressing his own flies as soon as possible. In the first place he should consider, apart altogether from the purely entomological and academic point of view, the appearance and ways of the live insect in its home. It is not advisable, for the growth of his own personal sense of things, that he should accept and copy piece-meal the well-known standard flies of other people. This method would be far too cramping in its effects on the natural, experimental attitude of glorious youth.

A gradual change has been coming about in the minds of thoughtful fishermen in regard to the appearance of insects as seen from below by the fish. The effect of reflected light in modifying

colour is in consequence now claiming a good deal
of attention.   There is plenty of room for research
in this direction.

If the beginner in fly dressing has no sympathetic
schoolmaster, like " Bob," to turn to at the com-
mencement of his career he cannot do better than
buy a book entitled " Brook and River Trouting,"
wr
H. Edmunds.   It describes the dressing of all the
typical northern flies.   The chapters on feathers
and materials are excellent.   The whole of the
book is eminently practical, as becomes a fisher of
Mr Edmund's calibre.

Young town-bred sportsmen can, if they are so
minded, follow up the study of the live insect by
visits to some of our entomological museums.   The
" set up " dead things will, of course, be found
wanting in one of their salient characteristics,
unceasing movement and tireless energy.   Nevertheless, there is a good deal to be learned by picking
out the typical fishing insects in the various cases,
and examining both their under, and upper, surfaces.   The general sobriety of their colour will be
found to be in striking contrast to those that are
often to be seen over-coloured in pictures.

My entomological friend, mentioned in connection with the note on " The Insect Food of Trout,"

is now the academic head of the kind of menagerie I am speaking about. In his case the severity of the usual scholarly manner is toned down by a liking for the sport of angling. In the days of his youth he pursued with boyish ardour the quest of all those little living things known as aquatic insects. I set him up as a kind of example. When " Bob's " apprentices were living their wild free days of foraging, by beck and dyke, he was always to be seen on more definite business bent, with some kind of net and case in his hands. Occasionally, however, it was a fishing net and pannier. It is this latter human touch which makes both men and boys " wondrous kind."

Nowadays I often climb to the top of a big University building to ferret him out. In some of his particularly local cases I can see many old Eden friends, and a few annoying foes. All manners and kinds of insects, however, are to be found there, " set up " with wings both spread and closed. They always interest me in spite of the confusing lists of their generic and specific names.

The student fisherman must there do as Rome does, but he need not necessarily study the various orders according to entomological law. It is taken for granted that he will not put the cart before the horse. His visit to museums will follow observation at the riverside. He will then have some idea in his mind as to what to look for; types of insect food that frequent his fishing beat.

Inquiry of this kind, on the river, and in the museum, will soon convince the thoughtful student that facsimile copying of nature, besides being impossible, is not quite the kind of thing that is wanted in artificial fly dressing. He will realise, too, from his studies, and from the lamp of experience, that flies made up of hooks, feathers and silk are as much creations of the mind as good pictures. That, although much has been said, written, and thought about them, the last word has yet to be said.

THE ALL-ROUND ANGLER'S RODS

THE man who fishes for pleasure, with all the lures mentioned in the various chapters of this book will probably be equipped with half a dozen rods. He may have as many more hanging on his rod rail, at home, but following the first six, in order of usefulness, the rest will only be of historic interest.

It is taken for granted that the first two serviceable rods, on the rack, will be fly rods.

The first of these two will be a trifle heavier and longer than the second, on the stiff side in balance and power. This is the rod for heavy stream work when the trout are lusty and full of fight. It is ten feet six inches long and weighs ten ounces.

The second rod is six inches shorter and two ounces lighter than the first, wherewithal stiff, and of quick action, suitable for summer-time fishing, with either a wet or floating fly—a rod that can be used all day without imposing any undue strain on the wrist.

The third is a light but strong general fly rod, nine feet six inches long and about seven and a half ounces in weight. An ideal rod for the angler who has discovered the joy of beck fishing. It is suitable for creeping and casting under trees, to right and left, in low underhand swings and jerks, with a short line, etc.

The fourth rod is eleven feet long and just over ten ounces in weight, light for its length but not wobbly, suitable for creeper and stone-fly fishing, and for worming when the water is low and clear in June. An extra six inches on the length of a rod makes an enormous difference in regard to both balance and effective fishing in clear water. This particular rod, reaches in length, the limit of single-handed casting power for the ordinary man. It should, therefore, be balanced to a nicety, with a reel of sufficient weight.

The fifth rod is seven feet six inches long, a light spinning rod of the famous Victor type, and suitable for use with a three and a quarter inch Silex, a two inch Malloch, or an Illingworth reel. Such a rod will " give " easily when the shock of striking with a minnow, on a fine trace, takes place, and neither break the gut nor wrench the small hooks out of the mouth of the fish.

The sixth rod is also for spinning, of the same

length as the fifth but stiffer and a trifle heavier, suitable for fishing in either a rising or falling flood, with a strong trace and larger minnow on a crocodile or somewhat similar tackle.

All the rods mentioned above are in two pieces. With such a set the all round angler is fully equipped for all the requirements of river and beck fishing for trout and grayling.

DESCRIPTION OF FRONTISPIECE PLATE OF FLIES

Row 1. Shows a set of eight typical Eden Flies. The numbers run from left to right.

No. 1.
Light Snipe and Yellow

DRESSING AND SEASON.

Small covert feather from under the wing of a snipe, body and head yellow silk.
Spring and Autumn, but a useful fly throughout the season.

No. 2.
Water-hen and Red

. Small greyish feather from the under coverts of a Waterhen's wing, body and head red silk.
Summer and Autumn.

No. 3.
Water-hen and Yellow

Ditto, body and head yellow silk.
An excellent fly throughout the season.

196

No. 4.	DRESSING AND SEASON
Partridge and Orange	Small mottled feather from the neck or back of a Partridge, body and head orange silk. One of the best spring flies. March, April and May.
No. 5. Blue Hawk . .	Small marginal covert feather from the upper side of the wing of a Merlin, body mole's fur ribbed with yellow silk. Season, March and April.
No. 6. Light Starling . .	Small covert feather from under the wing of a starling, body and head yellow silk. Season, July, August, September.
No. 7. Dark Snipe and Purple	Small marginal covert feather from upper side top of the wing of a Snipe, body and head purple silk. Season, March and April.
No. 8. Light Woodcock	Small covert feather from under the wing of a Woodcock, body and head yellow silk. Season, Spring, Summer, Autumn.

Rows 2 and 3 show examples of the more generally well-known flies which are useful on the Eden.

Row 2. No. 9.

Broughton Point	.	Season,	Early Spring.

No. 10.

Red Quill .	.	,,	May and June.

No. 11.

Greenwell's Glory	.	,,	March, April, May and September, but an excellent fly at all seasons of the year and very rightly famous.

No. 12.

Cairn's Fancy .	.	,,	April and May.

No. 13.

March Brown (Male) .		,,	End of March to beginning of May.

No. 14.

March Brown (Female)	,,	Ditto.

No. 15.

Iron Blue Dun .	.	,,	May and June.

Row 3. No. 16.

Brown Bustard		,,	June, a type of the artificial moths used in night fishing.

No. 17.

Black Spider .	.	,,	June, July and August.

No. 18.

Red Spider .	.	,,	May onward in coloured water.

No. 19.

Blue Dun .	.	,,	April and May.

No. 20.

Olive Dun .	.	,,	May and June.

No. 21.
Dun Midge . . Season, July and August.

No. 22.
Red Spinner . . ,, May onwards.

Row 4. FLOATING FLIES.

No. 23.
Whitchurch Dun . ,, June, July, August.

No. 24.
Medium Olive . . ,, Ditto.

No. 25.
Pale Watery Dun . ,, Ditto.

No. 26.
Iron Blue . . ,, Ditto.

Row 5. DOUBLE HOOKED
FLIES.

No. 27.
Snipe and Yellow . ,, March, April and
May in the becks.
No. 28.
Broughton Point . ,, Ditto.

No. 29.
Blue Hawk . . ,, Ditto.

Row 6. GRAYLING FLIES.

No. 30.
Red Tag. . . ,, September, October
and November.
No. 31.
Green Insect . . ,, Ditto.

No. 32.
Poult Blon   .   . Season, September, October, and November

No. 33.
Little Chap . . ,,   Ditto.

No. 34.
Apple Green Dun . ,,   Ditto.

No. 35.
Water-hen Bloa . . ,,   Ditto.

1   " DOUBLE HOOK," MINNOW TACKLE.   2   " DOUBLE HOOK," MINNOW TA
                                         BAITED.
3. WORMING TACKLE FOR GRAYLING 4   CROCODILE TACKLE, TROUT SIZE.
5. " THREE HOOK" WORMING TACKLE 6   CREEPER TACKLE BAITED (FIXE
    BAITED.   A PIECE OF CORK.
7   CREEPER TACKLE.   8   WORMING TACKLE.

(See also Supplementary Note No. 14.)

DESCRIPTION OF TACKLE PLATE

(From left to right)

No. 1 shows a " double hook " minnow tackle, on the Ariel principle, for fishing in clear water. The tackle is made up with fine 2X gut. The gorge lead is made out of one-eighth inch soft lead wire, cut to one and a quarter inches, and flattened slightly at the head, where the small holes for the insertion of the gut come, on opposite sides, and through the centre of the flattened top. The point is hammered, not filed, to the taper shown. The soft lead is bent to a curve for the production of " spin."

No. 2 shows No. 1 tackle baited.

No. 3 shows a worming tackle for Grayling (Hardy's side barbed hooks No. 14).

No. 4 is the well-known Crocodile tackle, trout size, also catalogued as No. 4.

No. 5 shows a " Three hook " worming tackle, baited.

No. 6 shows a creeper tackle baited. The bottom hook through the lower body or tail, length-wise, and the smaller top hook pricked into the thorax. (Top hook is fixed to cork for photography.)

No. 7 shows the creeper tackle. It is made up with a No. 2 eyed top hook, and a No. 3 tapered shank, bottom hook.

The stone-fly tackle should have a No. 4 hook at the bottom, otherwise the two tackles are identical.

No. 8 shows the worming tackle. It is made up with three No. 2 hooks, the top hook is eyed. The hooks are attached to a piece of strong natural gut, one and a quarter inches long (Marana 1st). This stiff gut holds both the tackle and the worm straight.

All the hooks used in tackles Nos. 5, 6, 7, and 8 are Hardy's Fly Hooks (1920 model), with wide gape.

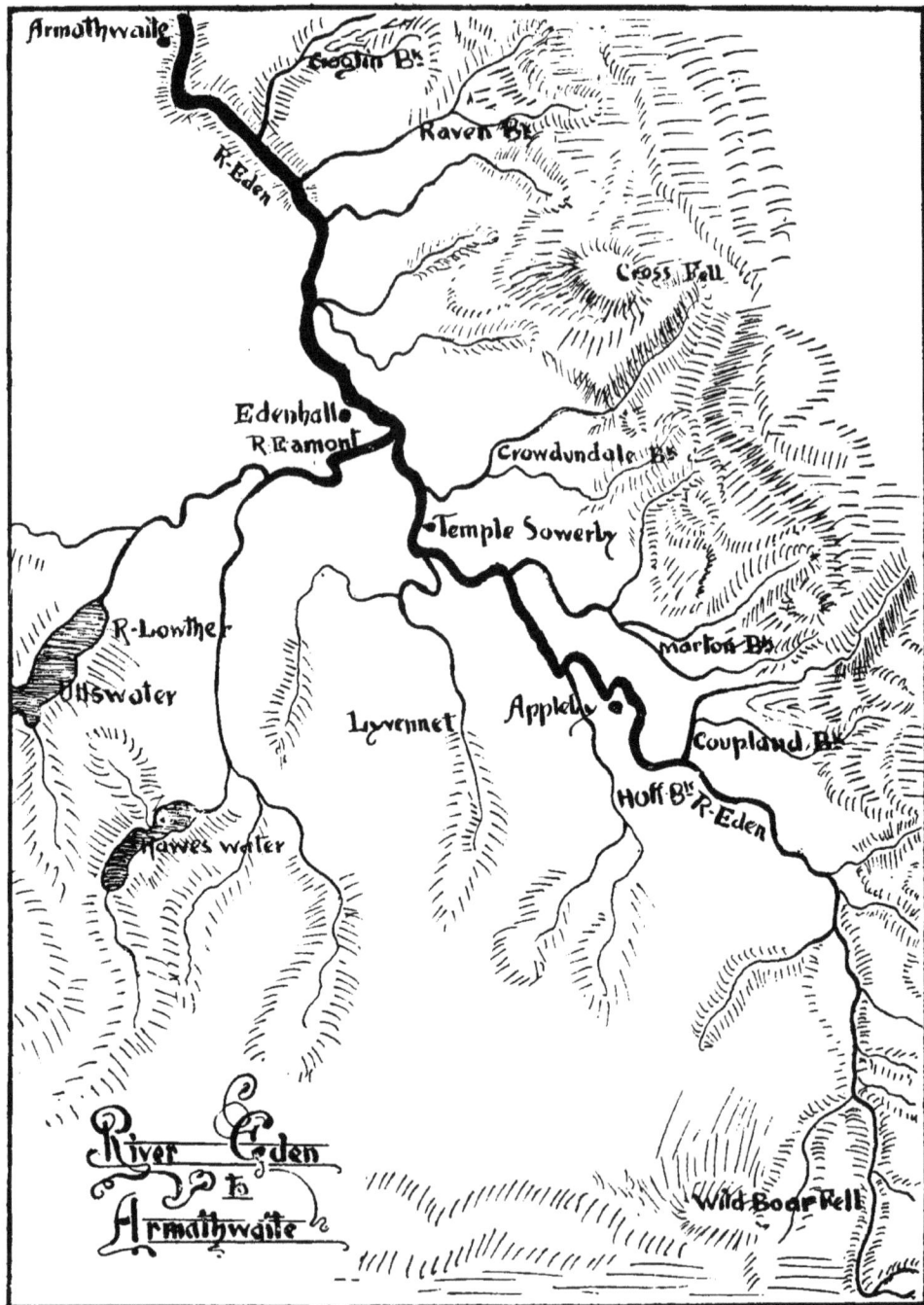

River Eden to Armathwaite

Labels on map:
Armathwaite
Goglin Bk.
Raven Bk.
R. Eden
Cross Fell
Edenhall
R. Eamont
Crowdundale Bk.
Temple Sowerby
marton Bk.
R. Lowther
Ullswater
Lyvennet
Appleby
Coupland Bk.
Hoff Bk. R. Eden
Hawes water
Wild Boar Fell

INDEX

203

9 781330 580127